DIGITAL BUSINESS GOLDMINES

The Hottest Profitable Internet Businesses You Can Start In Next 24 Hours With With Zero Investment, Zero Experience, And Zero Technical Skills"

DR. OPE BANWO

DIGITAL BUSINESS GOLDMINES FOR YOUNG NETPRENEURS

A Practical Breakdown Of Hottest Profitable Internet Businesses You Can Start in Next 24 hours With Zero Investment, Zero Experience, And Zero Technical

Important Legal Stuff

This book is © Dr. Ope Banwo. All Rights Reserved. You may not sell this book, give it away, display it publicly, nor may you distribute it in any form whatsoever.

While reasonable attempts have been made to ensure the accuracy of the information provided in this publication, the author does not assume any responsibility for errors, omissions or contrary interpretation of this information and any damages or costs incurred by that.

This book is not intended for use as a source of legal, business, accounting or financial advice. All readers are advised to seek the services of competent professionals in legal, business, accounting and finance fields.

While examples of past results may be used occasionally in this work, they are intended to be for purposes of example only. No representation is made or implied that the reader will do as well from using any of the techniques mentioned in this book.

The contents of this book are based solely on the personal experiences of the author. The author does not assume any responsibility or liability whatsoever for what you choose to do with this information. Use your own judgment.

Any perceived slight of specific people or organizations, and any resemblance to characters living, dead or otherwise, real or fictitious, is purely unintentional.

You are encouraged to print this book for easy reading. However, you use this information at your own risk.

About The Author

Dr. Ope Banwo, also known as the **'The Fearless Netpreneur'**, is an accomplished Entrepreneur, Attorney, Author, Motivational Speaker, Internet Coach and Corporate Solutions Provider. He holds several degrees in law including LL.B, B.L, LL.M and a PH.D. He was admitted to the Nigerian Bar in 1986; the New York Bar, USA, 1997 and Fed District Court of Nebraska, USA in 1997.

Dr. Ope Banwo believes the Internet presents unique opportunities for people all over the world to achieve their financial dreams.

As part of his efforts to help youths become self-employed on the internet, he organizes free seminars on how to harness the power of the internet to achieve financial freedom under his **Digital Works Academy** platform. He also offers ongoing coaching, mentorship, training and motivation for thousands people on how to make money online.

As a prolific author, Dr. Ope Banwo has written many books on different topics including internet marketing; social media marketing; Christianity and business management.

Some Of Dr Ope Banwo's best-selling books on internet business include **Confessions Of A guru Wannabe, Social Media Genesis, Digital Marketing Without Tears, Digital Business Goldmines, The Income Angel, Launchify360 Formula; Deadly Sins Of Social Media, 10 Deadly Sins Of A Product Launch**, etc

His non-profit organization, **Ghetto Dreamz Foundation,** and his **Internet Newbies Academy,** also provides ongoing scholarship, mentorship and training to help economically disadvantaged and at-risk inner city youths in actualize their dreams of success.

You can find out more about him and his business at his trademark blog: www.FearlessNetpreneur.com.

Some of the sites recently developed by Dr. Ope Banwo and his flagship company, Netpreneur360 Inc. include:

1. www.FearlessNetpreneur.com
2. www.DigitalMarketingWithoutTears.com
3. www.Webcommerce360.com
4. www.NetpreneurChamber.org
5. www.Netpreneur360.com
6. www.5kJobber.com
7. www.AmericanInternetBusinessSchool.com
8. www.Mobimatic.io

9. www.Livematic.com
10. www.DigitalWorksAcademy.com
11. www.Launchify360.com
12. www.ImRehabCenter.com
13. www.Webiference.net

INTRODUCTION TO DIGITAL BUSINESS GOLDMINES

It is one thing to understand that there is money to be made on the internet, It is quite another thing to know exactly where that money can be made.

In addition, any serious business person must seriously consider the Strength; Weaknesses; Opportunities and Threats (SWOT) inherent in each opportunity before making a choice which one to pursue.

While there are literally hundreds, if not thousands. of ways to make money on the internet, I will choose just 11 most promising ones to discuss in this chapter. The more enterprising NetpreneurS can then do more research to uncover other gems not mentioned in this manifesto.

This section is for those still looking to choose the right models for making money on the internet consistently.

Having considered some of the prevailing structural and practical factors, I will recommend about 11 different models that you can use to make money consistently on the internet. I will also share briefly with you some of the viable options for making money online. I will honestly share with you the Strengths, Weaknesses, Opportunities and Threats in each model, and it is up to you to pick the one that suits you, your talents and temperament the most before plunging into the internet money making efforts headlong.

CAUTION: Like everything else you need to get the proper foundation AND Knowledge about how business works on the internet before jumping in. There is nothing more frustrating for any new internet marketer than to jump into the business without having a solid understanding of how set up your own internet business.

I therefore strongly recommend that you register and take the Internet Newbies Academy Course at www.internetnewbiesacademy.com or register at the American Internet Business School to take the Certificate course on Internet Business Blueprint for Course.

Also, I strongly encourage you to start with ONLY ONE option and master that before trying other goldmines. You cannot dig in too many goldmines at the same time and expect to make any money. Focus all your energy, resources and time on ONE OPTION first. Make sure you are profitable before trying your hand on another field.

As I pointed out under the most common mistakes of Netpreneurs, lack of focus is a definite killer of dreams.

Consider yourself duly warned!

CHAPTER 1

DIGITAL BUSINESS GOLDMINE #1: BLOGGING

Blogging is one of the easiest models that anyone can attempt. Almost anyone can become a blogger. Even those who can't write can still blog with pictures.

A blog is a personal diary. A daily pulpit. A collaborative space. A political soapbox. A breaking-news outlet. A collection of links. Your own private thoughts. Memos to the world.

Your blog is whatever you want it to be. There are millions of them, in all shapes and sizes, and there are no real rules.

In simple terms, a blog is a website, where you write stuff on an ongoing basis. New stuff shows up at the top, so your visitors can read what's new. Then they comment on it or link to it or email you. Or not.

Since Blogger was launched in 1999, blogs have reshaped the web, impacted politics, shaken up journalism, and enabled millions of people to have a voice and connect with others.

And we are pretty sure that the whole deal is just getting started.

Strengths: You can blog about anything you want! Focus on your passion and share your thoughts with the world. If you have great content, people will come to your blog and you can monetize through advertising or affiliate programs. The start-up cost is only $9 and it costs about $5 a month to maintain this business model (You only pay for the domain name and monthly hosting respectively.) You can even register some blogs for free!

Weaknesses: It may take a long time to build up traffic – an average person who blogs regularly but slowly may quit his or her job within one to two years. If you want to achieve freedom in half the time, you have to blog and network with other bloggers more aggressively.

Opportunities: You may not be able to see yourself making money at the start, but to offset that, you can blog for others (for a fee) or even sign up for PAY PER POST and get paid for blogging!

Threats: There is a blog born or created every **TWO**

SECONDS. So you can imagine how much competition you are going up against!

There are countless examples of people who have become very wealthy through running a blog. Pat Flynn who owns (www.smartpassiveincome.com) is one such example. Pat is a guy who talks about making money online and who actually owns several blogs and websites including one aimed at food trucks which he publishes his earnings from. Pat's blog is very easy to read and provides a ton of great information and as a result, he has achieved almost superstar status and is invited to big events. This is just an ordinary family guy! Pat makes his money mainly through adverts on the sites and via sales of information products.

Another great example is The Art of Manliness (www.artofmanliness.com). This blog was founded by Brett McKay in 2008 and focusses on a range of topics relating to what it means to be a man in the 21st century. It's a unique niche that allows him to cover diverse topics ranging from beard trimming, to weightlifting, to how to smoke a cigar and drink whiskey. The site is now highly successful and provides far more than a full time income to Brett and his family. He makes his income through various types of advertising, possibly commission on physical products and through sales of his *own* products through an ecommerce store.

How to Get Started, And Succeed as a blogger!

In order for a blog to become profitable, it's often necessary for you to be getting hundreds of thousands of views a day *and* to have a smart form of monetization in place.

The question is, how do you get to this point?

Setting Up a Blog

Thankfully, actually setting up a blog is a relatively easy process. To do this, you'll need to find a hosting account and a domain name and you'll probably want to use a CMS such as WordPress.

A hosting account is basically what gives you the 'space' to store your files on the web. You'll be paying a monthly or yearly fee in order to rent space on a 'server' which is a giant computer that remains constantly connected to the web at all times. You place your website files on that and it ensures they're able to be served up when someone wants to find them.

In *order* to find those files though, your visitors will need to use your domain name or URL. This is the address that people will type in order to find your website and this address is going to point at the specific directory within the server so that people are shown your website when they navigate there.

Fortunately, finding hosting and a domain name are both relatively easy tasks and shouldn't set you back too much more than $200 a year to begin with (tops). This is where creating a SaaS business would be much more complicated – as you'd need a lot more space and speed from the server in order to let thousands of users upload and edit files as they needed to.

A great example of a hosting site that also offers domain name registration and web hosting is Blue Host (www.bluehost.com). A quick search on Google though will yield many, many more.

Next comes the CMS. CMS stands for 'Content Management System' and essentially what this is, is a tool that will allow you to easily change the look of your website and to add and delete pages of content.

The best known CMS is WordPress and it's *highly* recommended that you go this route. WordPress will allow you to create a website in minutes rather than months, it will manage your files and it will look highly professional. WordPress is not a 'beginners' tool by any means but rather is a professional piece of CMS software that is actually used by many of the biggest brands on the planet.

Huge websites like Forbes, the BBC and Mashable use WordPress, as do the aforementioned successful blogs we mentioned. Using WordPress also ensures your site will be compatible with a ton of useful tools and features including the aforementioned WooCommerce and Amember. It also means you'll have a community of people out there who can help with any technical troubles you may be having and that your site will be easy for most web developers to understand and edit. In short, WordPress makes life *much* easier for you and also makes your site far more professional. It is tried and tested and known to succeed… so why go with anything else?

If you choose a prominent hosting service like BlueHost, then the option to install WordPress will even be right there in the control panel meaning it takes literally just one click.

All that said, there *are* other CMS options if you would prefer. One is Joomla! (www.joomla.org) which is similar to WordPress and offers a lot of flexibility. It's a lot more fiddly though and there's less support available – mostly it is used in house for companies creating backend software. Another popular choice is Drupal, which is again much more complicated. Of course you could always create your *own* CMS or forego having one at all, but either of these choices will drastically increase your workload while actually putting your business at more risk.

Note: There are other options that don't require self-hosting, such as Blogger. However, this is an inferior tool for multiple reasons. Not only do hosted options mean you can't choose your own URL but they also tend to be very limited in terms of space, bandwidth and the other elements of your website. Blogger is also highly limited in terms of the features it offers for building your own web design. In other words, if you want to create a *proper* website with the potential to grow and scale into something that will earn a lot of money, you can't use something like Blogger.

Creating Blog Posts
Once you have your blog and you've given it a look and navigation you're proud of, the next step is to start writing blog posts. This is very important as it's what will give your site its value and it's what will encourage people to want to visit your site and hopefully to come back time and time again.

The problem though is going to be standing out in a sea of content from other websites and blogs. To do this, you need to focus on offering something that is very high quality and that is consistently offering value. As we'll see later on, this is also good for your SEO.

The key to remember is that someone has to *want* to read your content based on the title and based on their previous experience with your site and brand. If you constantly churn out content that is uninspired, derivative or badly written then no one is going to bother to visit.

This is why the 'optimal length' for a blog post is actually around 1,800 words. That might seem a bit long but this kind of length is what will enable you to really dive into a topic and to offer some insight and discussion that can't be found elsewhere. It lets you do a comprehensive overview of a subject and it lets you make your blog post into a resource that other people will recommend and share around the net.

Meanwhile, you also need to think about the title and the topic. If you are writing another article called 'Top 10 Pec Exercises' for your fitness website, then you aren't likely to win over any new fans. Why? Because this subject and structure have both been done to death already! People read the title and already know precisely what your post will be about and they've probably already seen the top ten exercises you're going to offer. How is that providing value?

On the other hand, consider the topics/titles from Maria Popova's incredible 'Brain Pickings' (www.brainpickings.org) website. Here are a few:

"Bruce Lee on Self-Actualization and the Crucial Difference Between Pride and Self Esteem"

"The Outsider With the Public Voice: How Joan Didion Mirrored Us Back to Ourselves"

"A year Without Mom: A Gorgeous Graphic Novel About Separation and Reunion, the End of Childhood and the Tradeoffs of Happiness"

These titles are unique, fascinating and they beg to be read. What's more, is that when you click on any of those titles, you quickly find that the same care and attention has been given to the posts themselves. Each blog post is between 1-3,000 words long, it is decorated by beautiful images and quotes and it is very well written. In other words, it's offering real value for the reader and giving them something to enjoy over a cup of coffee.

How much *more* likely do you think that something like this is to generate discussion? Or to get shared? And how much more likely is someone to subscribe to that blog? It's just *so* far superior when compared to an article on 'The Top 10 Pec Exercises'.

Of course this doesn't mean all your posts need to be highly thought-provoking philosophical pieces – they just need to be unique, inherently interesting and different.

If it's the fitness niche you're interested in, then consider some of these titles from Breaking Muscle (www.breakingmuscle.co.uk):

"World-Level Weightlifters Are Just Like Us"

"The One-Session, One-Exercise, One-Set Strength Plan"

"So, You Want to be a Lion?"

Again, all of these titles are interesting and unique and the posts are long, in-depth and provide tons of value. T-Nation (www.t-nation.com) also does this very well:

"Iron Core: How to Build a Punch-Proof Body"

"A Lifter's Guide to Alcohol"

You can even consider the 'clickbait' articles used to generate traffic via social media. These articles use titles like 'You'll Never Believe What This Mum Does Next… Shocking!" or they employ controversy. Either way, this makes the user curious and they want to click. You're objective is to generate that same curiosity but then to *deliver* on the promise in the title by making sure your posts are *actually* as interesting and unique as they sound.

And keep in mind too that the point is eventually to convert your visitors into paying customers. To do that you need to gain their trust and you need to demonstrate your ability to provide value. Once again, the best strategy is clearly to create content that is interesting, unique and in-depth.

> *The Fearless NetpreneurAdvise:*
> *Like everything else in life, to master this niche and start making serious money with it, you need proper training. I encourage you to sign up for the Pro Bloggers Club now at <u>www.probloggersclub.com</u>. It will probably be the best small money you ever spent!*

CHAPTER 1A

30 PROVEN WAYS TO MAKE MONEY WITH YOUR BLOG

As a new Netpreneur, just like other savvy bloggers from all over the world, there are many different ways to generate money with your website online.

Unfortunately, too many people often give up because at that present time they are not making any money at all. It takes time to build a blog site that will make you money, though with the right direction, planning and hard work this can be achieved quicker. It all depends on how you **monetize your blog**!

The following list is a collection of many of the different ways of making money with your website. Depending on what your website is about, a large number of these techniques can be implemented to earn you cash. However, you should not give up or get discouraged if one method does not work for you, just try a different one and build upon that!

The following list is by no means exhaustive but it is a good start. You can research and get more for yourself!

1. PPC and CPM Ad Networks

Pay Per Click (PPC) Advertising:
The best (and easiest) income sources for bloggers (especially those who are just starting out) are PPC ad networks. A PPC Ad network is an advertising program in which ads are placed on your blog and you are paid whenever your visitors click on the ads. Simple, isn't it? And Totally Passive. You just put the PPC ads on your blog (inside the content, sidebar, header or just anywhere) and then see the money coming in. But hold on, It does require you to get traffic to your blog.

The best PPC network, without any doubts, is Google AdSense. It is the highest paying network and shows content related ads only. There are many alternatives to AdSense but most of them either pay too low or have less relevant ads. Some good alternatives to AdSense are Chitika, Adbrite and Bidvertiser etc.

1. Pay Per Click Advertising

The best (and easiest) income sources for bloggers (especially those who are just starting out) are PPC ad networks. A PPC Ad network is an advertising program in which ads are placed on your blog and you are paid whenever your visitors click on the ads. Simple, isn't it? And Totally Passive. You just put the PPC ads on your blog (inside the content, sidebar, header or just anywhere) and then see the money coming in. But hold on, It does require you to get traffic to your blog.

The best PPC network, without any doubts, is Google AdSense. It is the highest paying network and shows content related ads only. There are many alternatives to AdSense but most of them either pay too low or have less relevant ads. Some good alternatives to AdSense are Chitika, Adbrite and Bidvertiser etc.

Pay Per Click (PPC) ads vary in profitability depending on the amount of traffic your website gets. Only a small percentage of people will click on these ads, so to earn a lot of money from them you will need a lot of traffic.

The click-through rate (CTR) of your visitors depends on the design of your website. Certain parts of your website pages are more valuable than others, so to increase your CTR these PPC ads can be placed there. For example, spaces at the beginning and end of articles/blog posts are highly visible, so by putting a PPC in these positions may increase the chances of someone clicking on one. If on the other hand you place these ads at the bottom of the page where nobody can see them, then nobody will click on them.

The cost per click (CPC) can also determine how much you are likely to earn from this type of ad. Adverts that display financial products or mortgages will generate you more income due to the higher price of the actual product, compared with perhaps children's toys. The former may pay you as much as $1+ for every click through by one of your visitors, whereas a click on toys may pay you only a few cents.

PPC ads are a good way to easily monetize your blog. However, to make serious money from them you will need lots of traffic.

2. CPM (Cost Per Mile) Advertising

Cost per Mile advertising (CPM) is similar to PPC advertising, however instead of getting paid on a per-click basis, you get paid according to the number of impressions (page views) you get. This is worked out for every 1000 impressions that it has. For example, a website that gets 200,000 page views per month that displays a $1 CPM ad will generate you $200 a month!

There are a number of different CPM providers out there that you can get ads from. Each varies on how much they will pay you, generally the better the provider the higher rate you will be paid. This is because the best providers have access to more and better quality advertisers that are willing to pay you more.

Just like PPC, CPM adverts can pay you more depending on where the advert is placed on your website. The higher the ad is placed and the bigger the ad is, will generally make you more money.

CPM adverts are beneficial for websites that have lots of traffic and a high page view per visitor ratio, but it is still a good option to consider when looking to monetize your blog.

NOTE: see LIST OF TOP 20 CPM NETWORKS YOU CAN LEVERAGE TO DIG GOLD BELOW at the end of this section. Many have managed to get some serious internet gold from these networks listed. Check them out!

3. Text Link Ads

This type of advertising allows you to place text based ads within the text of your articles. For example, if you are writing an article about certain software, you can place text-link ads within your posts that would refer your viewers to that particular product.

You can't just link to anything though, you need to sign up to that specific product affiliate advertising scheme (see '*10. Affiliate Marketing*' below) or you can sign up to a specialized provider who will automate the service.

4. In-text Ads

Very similar to the above text link ads, 'In-text ads' are adverts that are placed inside your text content such as articles or blog posts. You can sign up to an In-text advertising provider that will place sponsored links within your text. These are double underlined to make them stand out from other links, so that when a user moves the mouse over one of them a small advertising pop-up will appear. The user can then decide if they want to click on it, which will make you a small amount of money.

These types of ads are a bit more obvious than the previous type, which can put some people off. If used properly, they can be a good way to monetize your blog.

5. Advertising Widgets

This method is relatively new on the scene. An increasing amount of people are using widgets on their websites to generate some money. These widgets are designed so that they can be easily placed onto a website without any hassle, which display a mixture of PPC, text link ads and affiliate programs.

6. Advertising Space

You can monetize your blog by selling space on your website for advertisers to display a banner. This can be a very lucrative method as it allows you to cut out the middleman and charge what you want for other people to advertise on your site.

Generally these deals are worked out so that you display an ad for a fixed amount of time for an agreed fee with the advertiser. The downside of this method is that you need to commit time to manage the whole process with the advertiser and that your site needs to have a lot of traffic to be considered by advertisers.

7. RSS Adverts

If you have an RSS feed (which you should!) then you can follow in the footsteps of millions of other website owners and start placing ads on it.

Many RSS feed generators now offer this service, so that it is even easier to implement them. Some offer CPM or PPC advertising, however you could opt to do it yourself and offer to sell sponsored messages or banners directly on your feed.

You can find adverts for your RSS feed on [BidVertiser](#) that you can implement to monetize your feed, though [Google FeedBurner](#) lets you do this as well.

8. Pay Per Play (PPP) Audio Advertising

Pay per Play (PPP) are audio adverts that are played every time someone visits your website. The ads usually only last a few seconds, with the viewer unable to stop it. This creates a 100% conversion rate with unique visitors, so you get paid about $5 per visit, however this method is very intrusive and may turn off your visitors, making them less likely to make a return visit.

Another form of audio advertising that you could use is 'Podcast ads'. If you run a podcast on your website, perhaps a weekly update letting your listeners know everything that is new on your website, then you could choose to include advertising. I believe that this type is less intrusive than the former because your podcast would just seem like a short radio show with commercial breaks.

As long as you don't go overboard with the amount of adverts, then this may be a method that could use to monetize your blog.

9. Pop-ups/

Pop-ups are very common online, but they are also very annoying. Many people hate pop-ups and have pop-up blockers installed to stop them. However, if executed in the right way, they can work. Having a single pop-up on your website that only appears to new visitors may work. They grab the attention of the visitor on their first visit and after that they won't be bothered again by them.

Pop-ups do not necessarily need to sell products directly. You can use them indirectly to promote aspects of your website, for example PopUp Domination can be used to encourage people to sign up to your email list of tutorial course, or alternatively you can create a light box with Aweber.

Pop-ups can work if you make them less annoying to people. The more frequently they appear, the less traffic you will get coming back!

10. Affiliate Marketing

If done right this, method is a great way to monetize your blog. Many of the previous methods can be used as affiliate marketing methods, but often a review of a product can work just as well.

For example, if you have a gardening website you could research affiliate programs that contain products related to gardening. Perhaps someone wants people to advertise their new lawnmower product, you could write a blog entry 'What's the best lawnmower for my garden?' and at the end you could promote the affiliate product.

With this type of advertising, you can get a commission with every sale that resulted from your recommendation. You refer viewers from your site via recommendations, banner ads, text link ads, etc., which takes them to the product page. If they buy, then you get a commission. This is often worked out on a percentage of the sale price, maybe 10-20%, sometimes more (I've seen products offer up to 80% commission) depending on the individual product.

11. Product Reviews

Basically the same as Affiliate Marketing, but more obvious. You can write detailed reviews about products and publish them on your site. Obviously it is better to review products that are related to your website, as you are catering to your target audience. There is no point writing a detailed review about a solar panel for your roof, if your website is about scuba diving.

Many people can build a website solely around product reviews, writing about a variety of subjects such as, hotels, holidays, cars, gadgets, films, etc. If that product has an affiliate program, then you can make quite a bit of money from it.

12. Create & Sell Your Own Product

We are a society of consumers! If you have a product that you have made, then why not sell it on your website. Perhaps you are a software programmer and have designed an app to help people track stocks on their mobile phone. You could let people download it from your website for a small fee. Maybe your hobby is pottery and you want to sell off some of your work, then sell it on a website. If they are popular, there might be a full-time business for them!

The good thing about this is that compared with selling a product in a shop that has a small customer basis, online you have the world to sell your product to.

13. Write an eBook

Everybody seems to be writing an eBook these days, so why don't you give it a try. These have become very popular in the last few years with the introduction of commercial eReaders such as the Apple iPad and Amazon Kindle.

You could write an eBook about almost anything. Maybe you are good at DIY, you could write a book about renovating your house that people might find useful. You can then sell it through the Apple iStore or on Amazon.

You can sell it directly on your website as well! This way you get 100% of the sale price and you get traffic to your website. Selling your own eBook can be an excellent way to monetize your blog!

14. Write a Hardback Book

This could be a continuation from writing an eBook. If you are a good writer you could publish your book in Hardback or paperback form. You could sell this on your website and send a copy to buyers.

This method is usually only successful for authors that have an existing following. An author may have a successful book that they then build a website around to promote it to a global audience. It can work the other way however. Many people have built a successful blog first and then written a book that has sold well.

If you are a good writer then this could be a good option for you. You can then find a self-publishing site, such as iUniverse that lets you publish your very own book.

15. Write Tutorials & Guides

The internet is a great place to find information. Everyone searches for tutorials detailing how to do something. You are reading a guide yourself on '30 ways your website can earn you money' right now!

I myself know very little about cars, so I would find tutorials and guides useful explaining technical things that I don't know. For example, a guide listing 'Help on buying a new car' or 'How to service your own car' would be very useful.

Everybody knows something that they could teach to another, so why not write about it and publish it on your own website. If it's a particularly popular niche that you are writing about, then you could attract a lot of traffic!

16. Teaching Program

The next step from writing tutorials would be to create an online teaching course. You could charge people a membership fee (see #22) or a fixed amount for joining a course that you have set up.

These courses could be about anything and could include podcasts, videos, tutorials, etc. For example, you may be an expert photographer. You could set up a 2 week online training course detailing how to be a better photographer. You could make videos describing all of the different equipment that you might need, techniques that help achieve excellent quality photos, how to develop photos in a dark room, etc.

You need to make sure that the information that you offer to your paying customers is different to any free content that you offer on your site. You will receive a lot of complaints if you just charged people $100 for information that they just read in your free blog! You can only charge people premium prices for premium content.

17. Live Workshops

The next step from creating an online teaching course is to have a live workshop. Live workshops let you interact with your audience and find out what they like about your website. People who come to your workshops get to meet you and ask you questions face-to-face.

Many people find these types of workshops appealing as they can get so much more out of it, than just following an online tutorial. This is why some people are prepared to pay a lot of money to attend these workshops.

As well as charging people for a ticket, you can make money in other ways from these gatherings. You can promote your own products or books (See methods #12, #13 & #14) at the end of each workshop. If you invite guest speakers to attend your workshops, then you can also collect 50% of everything that they make from promoting their own products.

You can also record the whole event and upload it to your website afterwards, perhaps advertising a future workshop.

Workshops aren't hard to arrange. Many hotels have conference rooms that you can book for an event. Once booked, you have a date to promote to your readers of when the workshop is taking place. You just have to prepare some kind of presentation, and keep advertising your upcoming workshop.

18. Host A Webinar

Webinar's are basically a live workshop online. People go on to Webinar's to hear you talk about your specialist subject. This is great for people that live over-seas that can't get to one of your workshops.

You make money from Webinar's by charging an individual for a virtual seat on your presentation. They pay to watch you perform your presentation online and they can interact during the process.

Webinar's can incorporate power point presentations, web-cams, photos, microphones, polls, etc., making them fully interactive with your audience. Questions are usually left till the end of the Webinar, where each viewer has the opportunity to ask any questions that they want to you.

You don't have to charge your audience anything to view a Webinar that you are conducting. You could just use it as a marketing tool promoting your website, but the majority of people often host an initial Webinar for free and then charge people for the subsequent ones.

19. Be a Consultant

You could monetize your blog by offering consultancy in your specific niche. You need to have a large number of followers and have built a good reputation in your field for this method to earn you money. You can offer one-on-one consulting to people over the phone or via Skype for a fixed rate. People would be willing to pay a premium for this service as they are paying for your undivided attention for an hour or more.

For example, you have built a reputation as being an expert in health and fitness and have a successful blog talking about methods of weight-loss and healthy eating. You could offer a consultancy service, where for one hour a day people can arrange to talk to you via web-cam to plan out a personal tailored exercise regime. You might charge $100 for the hour and the individual might not need to contact you until the next month.

As previously stated, you do need a reputation for this to generate you any money. This is not a method for a startup website, but it could be something to aim for in the future as you grow your website.

20. Find Sponsors For An Event

If your website involves organizing events, such as a workshop (See Method #17), or a weekly podcast, etc., you could find companies to sponsor them. Then at the beginning and at the end you would have to promote the sponsor.

You see this type of advertising a lot on TV and in Sport. Many TV shows are sponsored to generate income.

The advantage of this method is that it gives website owners more options to monetize each aspect of their site. Advertisers are attracted to sponsorship deals on high traffic websites as it allows them to reach a targeted audience.

21. Selling Services (Hire Me)

This is often the reason why many people start a website in the first place. You might have a profession in the real world, such as a stock trader, architect, life coach, etc. You could build a website advertising your services to increase your client numbers. Visitors can pay for your professional services through your website and receive your help, as in the previous example this could mean full financial planning and strategies on stock trading.

Obviously, with this method you only get paid when you are working.

A great way to find clients is to <u>have your own 'Hire Me' page on your website</u>. That way, people can see that they can hire you to help them out.

22. Membership Site

Increasing numbers of sites offer premium membership areas. The most famous of these are Newspapers who are switching to more online content due to decreasing sales of actual newspapers. Websites attract visitors with free content and then they realize that they can get added benefits by paying a membership fee.

An example of this could be a 3D modelling website. The website could offer free tutorials, detailing step-by-step instructions on how to create 3D renderings of objects, perhaps a car. Paying members can download pre-made 3D models that they can use in animations, etc.

23. Private Forums

Similar to a paid membership, private forums can be created to cater to your audience. Members can pay an annual/monthly fee to access the forum and interact with the other members.

There are many free forums out there, so to charge members a fee to access your forum you need to provide excellent, individual content that isn't available elsewhere.

One example could be a networking forum where people can interact within a professional environment. A forum focusing on academic scientific research could attract scientists from around the world to collaborate with one another.

24. Email Marketing

Email marketing can generate you lots of money. The key is to build a large email list of your customers/visitors. When people register to become a member, you get their email address. When people sign up to your weekly newsletter, you get their email address. The more ways there are to get someone's email address the better.

With an email list, you can build a brand, recommend products, and promote any events/workshops that you may be holding and more importantly to can encourage people to keep returning to your website.

Email marketing isn't a direct way of making money, but it is a powerful way of increasing your income from your other methods by driving traffic back to your site. Just don't go overboard with emails so that they are viewed as spam! Nobody likes spam!

25. Surveys & Polls

You can place surveys and polls from certain companies on your website that will pay you for the privilege. You can sign up to these sites and choose a particular survey/poll that will fit in with the content on your website. Visitors of your site can participate in voting, whilst you get paid for displaying it. Most of these polls operate on a Cost per Mile basis.

26. Paid Directory Listings

This method is an alternate way of selling advertising. Unlike displaying adverts on a page, you allocate space on your website to list links to different companies and services that are related to your niche.

For example, a blog about graphic design could have a separate page that displays links to professional graphic design companies and freelance graphic designers.

You can charge for the privilege to display these links on your website. You can guarantee that the links will be seen by X amount of people per month and you can charge a monthly fee. If you had a list consisting of 500 people and charged them $5 a month, you would make $2500 per month!

27. Job Boards

An advancement of direct listings is a job board. You can create a web-page that allows companies to post job vacancies. You can charge a small fee for the listing and maybe even a small finder's fee if the job is filled by one of your viewers.

This method is very competitive, there are many job boards out there, so a small site will have a very hard time surviving. This could be a suitable method for a larger site, as the more traffic you have, the more listings you are likely to attract.

28. Sell Your Custom Template or Theme

If you have spent time making your OWN custom template or theme, then you can consider selling it. An increasing amount of people are making their own website, therefore there is a demand for more templates that people can use.

The amount of money that you can make from this method depends on your website skills. A high quality template can be sold for as much as $100+ but that is the top of the range themes. If you have a skill for making these then you could build a small business around making and selling them.

This website runs on a theme that was purchased. The professional themes at <u>Woo Themes</u> is a great place to buy high quality templates.

29. Donations

A method that a lot of people don't even think of, Donations can provide an alternate source of income from your website. You can get a donate button from <u>PayPal</u> to place on your site and ask people to donate a small amount to you for the service that you provide.

This method is a good way to generate some income if you have a small website, you could ask people to donate an amount to help you pay the upkeep of the website. This method can work for much larger sites as well, generally sites that offer helpful information to its users, can benefit from this method as it allows readers to donate a small amount of money if they feel that you have helped them in some way.

Some people may not like the idea of this, but the advantage of this method is that it can be easily set up and left. If people want to donate anything then they can, if not they don't have to. You'll be surprised how many people are willing to give you some money if you have genuinely helped them.

30. Auction Your Website

Some websites just don't make money for whatever reason, but before you just give up and walk away, you could consider selling your website. You can find many sites that offer to list your site for sale for people to bid on. You would be surprised to see how much some websites can go for.

Why would anybody want to buy your website? Well that is because people are lazy! It takes time and effort to build a website from scratch, so a lot of people like to buy built websites and build upon them. Some people do it for a living, building websites and then selling them on for a profit.

The advantage of this is that you can make quite a bit of money selling your website, it just depends on the quality of it.

> **The Fearless NetpreneurAdvise:**
> *Like everything else in life, to master this niche and start making serious money with it, you need proper training. I encourage you to sign up for the Pro Bloggers Club now at www.probloggersclub.com.*
> *It will probably be the best small money you ever spent!*

CHAPTER 1B

RESOURCES FOR GETTING THE INTERNET GOLD THROUGH BLOGGING

LIST OF TOP PAYING C.P.M NETWORKS FOR BLOGGERS

Below is a list of some of the top paying PPM networks that you can leverage to make money for you blog. Visit some of the sites and check out their rules and regulations and figure out how you can make money for your blog through them.

Like with everything provided in this book, please do your due diligence!

1. Tribal Fusion – Tribal Fusion is probably the best paying ads networking sites that makes use of e-CPM. Their network consists of most respected marketers wherein your profit is at highest level. Tribal Fusion is very simple to use and manage. It is possible to generate income from the clicks and make money handsomely. It offers 55% revenue sharing with check as the method for payment. $50 is the minimum cash out.

2. BidVertiser – You may make more income with BidVertiser on your own web or blog site. Earn money from each click. Just show the ads on your site and visitors may bid in opposition to each other and you are in the position to gain as a result. Bidvertiser shows the best bidder which means your income is maximized. Your earning will depend on the number of click. You may request payout of $10 minimum once a month via check payments.

3. <u>Technorati Media</u>: the largest social media advertising network. With deep agency and client relationships, they deliver targeted campaigns from top brands at high CPM. Technorati media has tie ups with many companies including Google, MSN, Yahoo!, IGN, Hearst, CNET, Tribal Fusion, Washington Post, and Time Inc.

4. Casale Media – Casale Media is a popular ad network of CPM with a very high reputation. Your gain could be as high as seventy percent profits share originating from solo banner ads that you apply on your own web site. Your income will increase by using Pop-unders. Casale Media offers the comprehensive support system that will help you with your inventory to make some revenue from your ads. This ad network offers 5 % for your second tier aside from the 70% revenue sharing. The payment method is by check or PayPal. The minimum payout is $25. Payment cycle is once a month.

5. Chitikas eMini Malls - When people visit your internet page for product advertising, Chitikas eMini Malls makes certain that your users click just after making planned choices on which to purchase. It's a powerful way to get the maximum results. You are able to pick your keywords or choose from a setting automatically. Chitikas eMini Malls can make your income grow with every click. This ad network offers 60% revenue sharing and 10% for the second tier. The payment method is via PayPal with a minimum pay out of just $10.00.

6. Admanage – With Admanage, advertisers and affiliates alike can easily generate income with pay per click (PPC) option. Their ad networks of search and display makes it possible for you to make more income from CPC Banners, Popup Ads, Text Ads, CPV Interstitials display ads and domain parking. You are able to increase your income with Ad manage. It offers 50 % revenue sharing and uses PayPal as the payment method as well as check and wire transfer. The minimum cash out is $100.

7. **Advertising**: Advertising.com is part of AOL. Advertising is also among top CPM ads network and also one of the high paying CPM rates. To join advertising.com you must have high visitors base.

8. **Burst Media** - Burst Media gives you high CPM's, quality campaigns, and full control of which ads run on your site. Your site must have minimum traffic of 25,000 monthly page views or 5,000 monthly unique views.

9. **CPX Interactive:** CPX Interactive was named 6th fastest growing privately held US advertising company in 2008 by Inc. Magazine for their annual list of corporate success stories. They deliver true scalability and transparency.

10. **Ad4game** – Ad4game is a uniquely developed high yielding eCPM ad advertising |company. It provides great advantages for publishers making use of a variety

of beautiful ad platforms to select from. Visitors are at its peak and so is also your income. You earn from every click and your income will surely increase. Content material is distributed on gaming sites to draw in more personalized visitors that bring you additional advantage. Earnings from Ad4game can be requested every 30 days via PayPal or wire transfer. There is no minimum payout.

11. **BannerConnect:** BannerConnect has been an expert on automated ad trading since 2004 and was one of the first companies in the world active on an ad exchange.

12. **ValueClick Media:** ValueClick Media is the premier Internet advertising network for publishers who wish to earn the most for their available inventory. You get the complete control over your advertisements along with quality advertising and superior support.

13. **Adtegrity:** Adtegrity.com, Inc. is an online advertising network with reach into over 30 vertical content channels specifically segmented for maximum impact with advertiser campaigns. For the publisher, the company follows the criteria that you need to have minimum 500,000 pageviews per month and your 50% traffic must originate from U.S. Moreover your site

should reside at a top level domain name that you own or control without any unlicensed material.

14. **AdPepper:** ad pepper media is one of the leading, independent international online advertising marketers. You can collaborate with ad pepper and can get comprehensive set of opportunities to market online presence profitably, whether national or international in scope. The company also offers weekly payouts.

15. **adBrite:** adBrite is the largest independent ad exchange, reaching 300 million global unique visitors every month, including more than 150 million in the U.S. adBrite's Exchange provides a yield management solution with advertisers being ranging from small local companies to world-wide advertising agencies. adBrite makes it easy for you to have access to thousands of advertisers with minimal effort. It supports different ad formats and provides publisher, the full control and account management.

16. **Vibrant Media:** Vibrant is the world leader in premium contextual technology aligning billions of words across the Internet. It has over 6,000 premium publishers, reaching over 250 million unique users per month, Vibrant offers publishers' premium editorial

tools to re-circulate users throughout their websites. You can gain incremental revenue through relevant display advertising and moreover, Vibrant Interest AD (VIA) are targeted based on words bought by brand advertisers, not by site with easy implementations.

17. **Axill:** Axill is one of the fastest growing publisher networks. Axill provides a complete solution for publishers to generate huge revenue from their websites by offering the best offers. You get the quality advertisers and you can track them with easily. You can earn effective CPMs possible and get paid on net 30 via Moneybookers or Wire Transfer.

19. **Clove Network:** Clove Network is an ad network that delivers services to thousands of high quality publishers. Clove network has a wide range of ad formats and solutions with flexible and transparent pricing model. They campaign top brands with optimized technology.

20. **Adify:** Adify owned by Cox Digital Solutions provides compelling solutions connecting advertisers with engaged users and publishers with quality brands. Company has built a suite of publisher services that maximize ad revenue and allow for greater operating

efficiencies. The company allows you to increase ad revenue, extend your reach, or take advantage of our industry-leading end-to-end platform.

CHAPTER 2

DIGITAL BUSINESS GOLDMINE #2: AFFILIATE MARKETING

Affiliate marketing is one of the most lucrative models on the Internet. Major companies like Jumia.com and konga.com have been creating awareness about this online money making goldmine with their heavy online and offline adverts. Savvy people are already picking up on this to make a huge windfall while others are still napping.

What is Affiliate Marketing and How to start with it? Affiliate marketing is a marketing practice in which a business rewards one or more affiliates for each visitor or customer brought about by the affiliate's own marketing efforts. As an affiliate, you can promote other people's product and get commissions for your efforts without seeing a single customer or talking to anyone.

My own simple definition is this: "Affiliate Marketing is promoting other people's (Company's) product and earning a commission in return (If a sale is made)." It works the same as in the offline world, however the profit and scope is much bigger over the Internet (Not to mention that people had exploited this too much though).

So basically what you do as an affiliate is: You promote other people's (or Company's) Product using a special link with a code only being used by you embedded into it (this is required by advertiser to track the leads referred by you).

If someone buys that product (or in some cases completes a task like signing up or completing a survey) using your link, it gets tracked by the advertiser and you are rewarded a commission (which is a percentage of the sale price but can also be a fixed amount as set by the advertiser).

This way both the advertiser, and the publisher, benefit. Advertisers get more sales of their product when many publishers (or affiliates) promote their product and Affiliates in turn generate revenue by promoting the product. Moreover Advertiser pays only when a sale is made so there is no risk of getting non converting visits like in some PPC campaigns.

This is the reason why most of the product creators and Advertisers provide an affiliate program for increasing their product sales.

Strengths*:* You don't even need a domain name or a website in some cases. You can earn huge commissions from up to 50% to even 100% commissions! You don't need to focus on creating products – just drive traffic to the merchant site and watch your income roll in (if you do it right of course).

Weaknesses*:* You will need to search for a good affiliate program and build up traffic in order to see results.

Opportunities: There are unlimited opportunities because there are always new products coming out each day and affiliates are needed everywhere!

Threats*:* You are competing against THOUSANDS of affiliates out there and those affiliates are your competitors. Some programs even offer two-tier programs and established affiliates probably have dozens of affiliates under them as well.

How To Get Started With Affiliate Marketing

There are a few things to keep in mind before choosing to get into this business. Firstly, you must find the right Affiliate Product to Promote and secondly you must have an audience that will be interested in that product.

Finding the Right Affiliate Product

This is the most Important Step (literally). If you get wrong here, you will definitely fail in this business. You will have to choose a product which will help your audience. If you have a Weight Loss Blog, then promoting a forex product will be completely useless as it will not get you any sales. Moreover, If you promote a low quality product (let's say, on your blog), you could be hurting your brand as well.

Remember, to get the best results, always promote a product that you have tried yourself or you must be confident enough of the quality of it.

Below are some of the tips that will help you find a related Affiliate Products:

Browse Affiliate Networks – The easiest way to get started with promoting products is to search though Affiliate Networks. An Affiliate Network act as an intermediary between publishers (affiliates) and merchant's affiliate programs. There are a few affiliate networks that list many affiliate programs. You can use their search option to get related products to your blog's niche. Some of the most famous Affiliate networks are: ClickBank (This is my favorite and also, the first affiliate commission that I earned was by promoting a ClickBank product), Commission Junction (aka CJ), ShareaSale etc.

Search Google – Other way to find relevant affiliate product that you can promote is by doing a simple Google search. Just type: "your keyword + Affiliate Program" (Replace "your Keyword" with your niche like "Weight Loss Affiliate Programs") and you will easily find the appropriate product.

Checkout Online Stores – Almost all of the famous online stores (like Amazon, EBay) have affiliate programs. You can just sign up for that and then promote any of the stuff that is listed there. Generally the commissions are not big here but as these online stores have a huge range of products; it is not that difficult to get referral sales through them.

Check Your Competition – If you can't find the products by above methods, you can simply have a look at what your competitors (sites in your niche) are promoting and you can start promoting those products.

Now, these are some of the ways by which you can select a product to promote.

You can make serious money promoting products as an affiliate in many way including: using your Blog; Social Networks; Writing and Submitting Articles: Creating Videos; Creating Web 2.0 Properties; Joining Online Forums: Building an Email List; and Creating Niche Sites

How to Get Started In Affiliate Marketing
So how does this actually work?

To begin with, you need to find your product that you want to sell. The easiest way to do this is through an affiliate network such as JVZoo (www.jvzoo.com), Commission Junction (www.cj.com), ClicBank (www.clickbank.com), WSOPro (www.warriorforum.com/warrior-special-offers/) or others.

Here, you'll then be able to find a massive list of affiliate products along with the amount they've sold, the commission they're offering and their price. You then find something that appeals to you and that fits your niche and you apply for an 'affiliate link'. That link is basically a special URL that directs people to the page where they can buy the product while also storing a cookie on their computer to show that you sent them. If they click your link and then buy the product within a certain time frame, it is logged as your sale and you get the money. Very straightforward!

The ClickBank Marketplace

Your job then is to simply promote that affiliate link, which you can do in a number of ways. You might for instance decide to simply set up an advertising campaign using Facebook Ads or AdWords. As long as you're paying less for the advertising than you're earning from the sales, then this will be an effective method.

Another option is to use your own channels. If you create a large email list then you can send your affiliate link around those subscribers after you've built their trust. Or if you have a blog, you can promote the link that way. You can even promote the links via social media, or using 'real world' posters and flyers. Or how about a YouTube channel?

Either way, this is a very simple and straightforward business model that lets you earn big cash without having to invest anything or take any risks yourself. There are some very well known figures in the affiliate marketing industry which include the likes of John Chow (www.johnchow.com) who is now somewhat famous online and regularly attends talks and interviews. Other big names include Mark Link and Rae Hoffman. All these people now live incredible lifestyles enjoying passive income while they travel the world or spend more time with their families.

Affiliate Marketing Best Practices And Tips
Now you know what affiliate marketing is and how to get started with an affiliate marketing network, the next thing to consider is how best to *succeed* in this space and to really start generating the kind of income you're looking for.

One of the most important points here is to pick the right product. Of course this means that you should choose a product that is selling well and that offers large commission on an attractive price point.

But on top of that, you also need to think about *how* you're going to sell that product and succeed in that niche. This is the most important part and it's something that will help you in a ton of different online business models actually.

When selling anything, you need to look for what is known as the 'route to market'. This essentially means the route you're going to take to present your product to the largest number of people who may be interested in it. If you have an eBook on flow arranging, then a route to market might be something like a blog on flowers, or maybe a magazine for brides-to-be.

Most of us have a few contacts and resources we can already use. Maybe you happen to be in touch with a big blogger in the fitness niche? Maybe you happen to know the editor of a magazine? Instead of choosing a random product and then trying to build that audience from scratch, choose the subject that you already have a headstart in and then exploit those contacts and opportunities. When you choose your product remember that you aren't *just* choosing your product – you're choosing your market, your marketing strategy and your audience!

Oh and often this means going for slightly smaller niches. It's sometimes easier to find and connect with a group of truckers than it is to get noticed among all the different marketers going after the dating crowd. Once again, starting small and building up is often the best strategy.

Physical Products?

One last point to consider is that there *are* also a number of affiliate programs aimed at people who want to sell physical products. The best known of these is Amazon's Associate Program (https://affiliate-program.amazon.com/) This lets you promote any product on Amazon for commission, potentially opening you up to a much wider audience. Bear in mind though that these sales offer *much* smaller commissions – typically about 3-10% of the retail price.

TIP FOR THE SERIOUS DIGGER:

For in-depth professional Knowledge and Training on how to become Certified to mine this internet income goldmine, visit American Internet Business School at www.ibsamerica.org . Click here to register for an ONLINE OR OFFLINE course for <u>Certificate course In Affiliate Marketing.</u>

CHAPTER 2A

LIST OF TOP 65 AFFILIATE NETWORKS IN USA AND EUROPE

There are countless affiliate networks out there where you can find products to promote for commissions ranging from 10% - 90% of the sale price. You can make a tidy income from these networks by signing up to promote products or by listing their products on your websites and blogs.

Below is a comprehensive list of some of the most profitable affiliate networks based in USA and Europe

TOP 50 AFFILIATE NETWORKS IN THE USA

1. **Commission Junction** Commission Junction, a ValueClick company, delivers performance-

based online marketing solutions. Network access to the USA, UK, Germany and France.

2. **LinkShare** US LinkShare pioneered online affiliate marketing, and today runs one of the largest pay for performance affiliate marketing network on the Internet. Network access to the USA, UK, Canada and Japan.

3. **ShareaSale** Established in 2000, Shareasale.com began on the premise that they could provide any merchant – large or small – with high quality, reliable tracking software – at a lower cost than the industry norm – with the added benefit of being plugged into a large network of affiliate sites.

4. **Share Results USA** An online affiliate marketing network. They provide the software, support and management services to help merchants drive targeted web traffic and sales to their retail websites. Network access to the USA, Canada and the UK.

5. **AdCommunal** A global CPA ad network catering to US and International traffic. We specialize in easy lead gen campaigns within the entertainment, education, and financial verticals

and feature many branded and high converting education, dating, finance, MMO games, email submits, and Zip submit campaigns. AdCommunal also boasts many tools for websites to monetize their traffic even further by providing offer feeds, peel away ads, interstitial ads and ad widgets to name a few.

6. **AdsMarket.com** Offers affiliates pay for performance programs from all over the world, including CPL, CPA and CPC offers. AdsMarket aim to try harder and outperform every chance they get to prove how sincere and earnest they are about putting more cash into your pocket.

7. **Advent Motive** Advent, Motive's flagship performance advertising application, was designed to maximize publisher's revenue, save them time and promote better user experience in the affiliate marketing space. Motive Interactive's groundbreaking lead generation platform, Advent allows publishers to launch streamlined campaigns with easy-to-use tools. Motive also ensures that you'll be provided with accurate and reliable payouts, exclusive campaigns, and attentive customer service.

8. **Advertising.com** Advertising.com conducts strategic direct-response and brand marketing campaigns that guarantee bottom-line results for their clients.

9. **affiliate.com** Was built with the goal of helping you grow your business and drive .

10. revenue. We are truly only successful when you are successful. As a network, we offer world-class affiliate support, top performing offers in a wide variety of verticals and some of the best value added services available. Redirect.com (International Monetization), The Parking Place (Domain Parking), DataOverdrive (List Management) and Dynamic Dolphin (Domain Registrar and Hosting Services).

11. **Affiliate Commission** Dedicated to providing a low-cost, effective "Pay Per Action" marketing network. Network access to the USA and UK

12. **Affiliate Fuel** Affiliate Fuel is a large affiliate network, with a record for performance and service. Helping advertisers and publishers work together to create promotions that are exciting, enticing, well-managed, fair, and profitable for everyone involved.

13. **Affiliate Future US** One of the UK's largest affiliate marketing networks, also active in the USA. Lead advertisers include Singapore Airlines, MatchClick, WorldSoccerShop and more.

14. **AvantLink** was founded in 2005 on the ideas of innovation, quality and service. They offer advanced and integrated Affiliate marketing tools including dynamic data feeds, RSS feeds, coupon feeds, product displays, and ad syndication options.

15. **Check My Stats US** An online provider of performance based marketing and sales solutions. Network access to the UK, USA and Australia.

16. **ClickBank.com** is a secure online retail outlet for 110,000 active affiliate marketers and 12,000 digital product vendors. ClickBank processes about 26,000 digital transactions a day or one every 3 seconds. And they pay affiliate marketers on time, every time. ClickBank does business in more than 200 countries worldwide.

17. **clickXchange.com** Provides pay for performance marketing custom affiliate programs for

marketing firms, consultants and individual in house affiliate program managers. An all-inclusive turnkey solution featuring, hundreds of programs and thousands of pre-screened affiliates.

18. **clixGalore USA** Offers five scaled levels of Affiliate recruitment and promotional services to our Merchants. Network access to the USA, Japan, Australia, India and the UK.

19. **CommissionSoup** provides e-business marketing solutions through their performance-based affiliate network. They offer a variety of programs and a complete line of services to ensure marketing objectives are met. CommissionSoup offers marketing material to accurately promote any program, advanced tracking systems, detailed reports, multi-site tracking options and monthly, dependable payouts.

20. **CoProsper network** A core focus on a dating and gaming with a range of CPL and CPA deals. Offers "daily" pay outs to top affiliates.

21. **CX Digital Media** CX Digital Media is a two-tiered CPA Affiliate Network with high-paying affiliate programs and top quality affiliates.

22. **Dark Blue** Affiliate network focused on providing the best affiliate programs from the top advertisers online.

23. **DigitalGrit** Gain access to the best merchants, outstanding customer service and most importantly, make your web properties more profitable

24. **Digital River** Affiliates earn up to 75% commission as participants in this affiliate network, powered by RegNow. Choose from the largest selection of software including games, anti-virus, and anti-spam titles.

25. **Direct Track** part of the DirectResponse Technologies, Inc. family of services. If you are a merchant looking for an affiliate and keyword tracking solution, an Agency looking for a private label affiliate and keyword tracking solution for your clients, or you are a Savvy Marketer seeking a solution to power your own Affiliate and Ad Network – then DirectTrack® is for you!

26. **Floppybank Network**. Floppybank understands the tremendous marketing opportunity that the Internet presents, and the importance of

independent marketplace to allow fast and effective transactions between advertisers and publishers.

27. **HasOffers Affiliate Tracking Software** HasOffers is an affiliate tracking platform SaaS that enables thousands of brands to create and manage their own affiliate programs. This simple, safe and scalable technology allows brands to track affiliates and effectively connect to new customers online. A complete API makes HasOffers a highly flexible solution for any online marketing strategy.

28. **Ice Water Traffic** Ice Water Traffic is run by AdBlink offering email marketing, lead generation and CPM based ad campaigns.

29. **Impression Up** Impression Up is an ad network that contains relationships with websites catering to the most sought after demographics. Their focus is as precise as their client requirements, aiming to achieve a return on investment through customer service and a track record for results.

30. **IncentReward Affiliate Network** Provide quality traffic to their advertisers through their affiliate base. Affiliates and Advertisers can both

enjoy quality service and customer support with dedicated account managers. For incentive affiliates they provide tools in order for you to reach a high commission volume through them. They welcome anyone large or small to apply to their network.

31. **Kowabunga!** Part of the Think Partnership family, creates online marketing products and services for the performance marketing industry. Together with top-notch customer service, an expansive and dynamic network and world-class tracking and conversion tools, KowaBunga! enables clients to increase revenues, drive traffic across multiple channels, create partnerships with new and existing customers and measure success. See also The KB! Open Network at Kolimbo

32. **Lead Crunch** A highly selective advertising network providing a quality "Pay for Performance" solution to advertisers and a reliable revenue source to publishers. Lead Crunch operates on the cost per action model to ensure our advertisers get the results they demand.

33. **Leadhound.com** A network of affiliate sites that will promote your site in exchange for payment when you get the desired results.

34. **LinkConnector** An affiliate marketing network, helping merchants and affiliates increase online sales. LinkConnector offers all standard affiliate program benefits, but is also changing the face of affiliate marketing to better meet your expectations.

35. **LinkRads.com** A Cost per Action (CPA) affiliate network. At LinkRads.com, we provide quality traffic to our advertisers through our vast affiliate base. Affiliates and Advertisers can both enjoy quality service and customer support with dedicated account managers, We welcome anyone large or small to apply to our network.

36. **MaxBounty** The mission of the MaxBounty Network is to put the money back where it belongs – in the hands of affiliates. MaxBounty accomplishes that mission by offering great campaigns at the rates that affiliates deserve.

37. **MyReferer** provides tools to run and manage your own affiliate program and can provide recruitment and management services.

38. **Netklix.com** Acting as the trusted third-party between the Advertiser and Publisher web-site,

Netklix.com tracks and reports transactions generated by visitors to the Advertiser web-site resulting from advert click-throughs on the Publisher web-site. Offers payouts in GBP(£), Euro and USD($)

39. **NeverblueADS.** At NeverblueADS, focus is bringing advertisers and publishers together. Leveraging their experience and longstanding relationships within the online marketing arena, they partner with top-tier advertisers to ensure that their network gets the most out of every impression.

40. **OfferForge USA** Forging lasting relationships. OfferForge have built a network based on bulletproof tracking and hosting, centralized real-time reporting, attentive account management, regular fast payouts and some of the best converting offers in the market. Each offer is carefully evaluated by their Affiliate Publisher forum to ensure suitability for inclusion.

41. **OffersQuest** An affiliate network owned by eMedia Quest, operating off of a private label Direct Track solution.

42. **OfferWeb.com** OfferWeb is set to permeate the internet market with leading technology, real-time reporting, and deep distribution channels.

43. **Performics** Now owned by DoubleClick, provides performance-based online marketing services and technologies for leading multi-channel marketers. Clients benefit from Performics' custom approach to affiliate marketing, search engine marketing and lead generation programs.

44. **PrimaryAds** A "Pay for Performance" network that specializes in cost-per-action advertising.

45. **Red Galoshes** A network focused on e-commerce sites designed, owned and managed by Red Galoshes. The network is private for their merchants but allows affiliates from all areas. There are around 25 merchant sites in the network

46. **Search4Clicks** provides publishers with the opportunity to earn significant extra revenue from un-sold ad space. Our programs provide some of the most lucrative CPL and CPA campaigns currently being run on the Internet.

47. **shop4affiliates** is a US focused network that is open to US publishers only.

48. **Webgains** Formed in 2004 to create a serious and professional presence in the on-line marketing arena. Webgains offers world-class customer service supported through experienced telephone support and on-line ticketing system. Their technology is developed in-house. Also operates in Europe.

49. **Websponsors** Established in June of 1998, as a dynamic Web-based advertising network offering primarily the Cost-Per-Action (CPA) revenue model. Websponsors serves as the core-lead acquisition product for Webclients, Inc., providing advertising customers with access to Web sites representing 29 different product categories.

50. **XY7.com** Offers you many top exclusive deals not found anywhere else on the net. Use these offers to maximize your revenues and list demographics, and never let unsold inventory go to waste.

TOP 15 AFFILIATE NETWORKS IN EUROPE

51. **LinkShare UK** LinkShare pioneered online affiliate marketing, and today runs one of the largest pay for performance affiliate marketing network on the Internet. Network access to the UK, USA, Canada and Japan.

52. **Advortis** A CPA network targeting UK and Europe for a range of CPA/CPL campaigns in verticals such as Gaming, Finance, Education, Autos Sweepstakes and competitions.

53. **Affiliate-Advantage** Core business is managing the relationship between affiliates and merchants so that affiliates can trust that they will earn money from promoting merchants.

54. **Affiliate Commission** Dedicated to providing a low-cost, effective "Pay Per Action" marketing network. Network access to the USA and UK.

55. **Affiliate Window** One of the United Kingdom's foremost affiliate marketing companies, with an emphasis on providing cutting edge technology and tools to maximize the return for on-line marketing programs.

56. **Buy.at** An advanced affiliate network connecting major UK retailers and merchants with the leading UK affiliate marketers.

57. **Check My Stats UK** An online provider of performance based marketing and sales solutions. Network access to the UK, USA and Australia.

58. **clixGalore UK** Offers five scaled levels of Affiliate recruitment and promotional services to our Merchants. Network access to the USA, Japan, Australia, India and the UK.

59. **DGM-UK** dgm, one of the UK's first and most experienced affiliate network specializes in affiliate marketing and search engine marketing. Their clients have been delighted by their ability to make performance marketing work for them for 10 years.

60. **MoreNiche** With most offers paying between 30-50% commissions, there might be no better place to start your affiliate marketing career.

61. **Profitistic** Is dedicated to delivering successful affiliate marketing campaigns on a Pay for Performance basis. This is achieved by providing cost-effective solutions for merchants and

offering quality offers to its base of affiliates and website publishers.

62. **Qwertytrade** QwertyTrade.com and many of its merchant web sites are owned by Spectra Ltd. Affiliate programs are pay per click systems that pays web affiliates for every unique visitor referred from their web site to a merchant site.

63. **Share Results** An online affiliate marketing network. We provide the software, support and management services to help merchants drive targeted web traffic and sales to their retail websites. Network access to the USA, Canada and the UK.

64. **TradeDoubler** A leading European provider of online marketing and sales solutions, TradeDoubler can offer a broad range of solutions from technically advanced and hosted management tools, to efficiently administered products within performance-based marketing. Network access to Austria, Belgium, Denmark, Germany, Spain, France, Ireland, Italy, Latvia, Netherlands, Norway, Poland , Switzerland, Finland, Sweden and the United Kingdom

65. **Webgains** Formed in 2004 to create a serious and professional presence in the on-line marketing arena. Webgains offers world-class customer service supported through experienced telephone support and on-line ticketing system.

CHAPTER 3

DIGITAL BUSINESS GOLDMINE #3: FREELANCE SERVICES

[Sell Your Services Globally And Mint Money]

The fastest way to make money online – offer your services as a freelancer based on your core competencies and earn money immediately by cashing in on your expertise!

Strengths: Fast and good money if you have the right clientele. In fact, this is one of the fastest ways to quit your full time job – just become a freelancer and be the boss of your own time!

Weaknesses: You need to have a skill and market your services. You have to build up your clientele as well and have them recommend more business to you.

Opportunities: Writers, graphic designers and other talents are in demand especially on the Internet.

Threats: You are competing against other freelancers, many of them sell their services TOO CHEAP!

The Internet has a market for everything. Even for your own services. If you think you are good at something, the Internet could be the best place for you to vend your skills. There are people looking for all kinds of services on the Internet. The jobsites have made the Internet a closer marketplace than any other. People are looking for services, and providers of these services are looking for people who they can sell the services to. The correct collaboration could mean a lot of money to you.

Of course, it is understood that the kind of services that have a demand on the Internet are services that you can provide online. These are mostly services related to website building and marketing. The following services are very much in demand:-

- Article Writing and Content creation
- Internet Research
- Blog management
- Search engine optimization
- Graphics Design
- Website Development
- Social networking services
- Proofreading and editing
- Video Creation

If you feel you fit within any of these skills, you could make an amazing amount of money with them.

Remember that the Internet allows you to reach out to a global level and you could liaise with people from all over the world to seek work.

CHAPTER 3A

TOP 40 FREELANCING SITES

The following are some sites where you can join and create an account quickly so that you start earning through this mode:-

1) Odesk.com – general
2) Freelancer.com – general
3) Freelance.com – General
4) Elance.com – general
5) 99designs.com – design
6) 5kjobber.com – a special Fiverr clone for africa
7) Guru.com – general
8) afridesk.com – general freelancing site
9) zulugig.com – general micro job site
10) Suite101.com – writing
11) Designcrowd.com – design
12) Freelanceswitch.com – general
13) Donanza.com – general
14) Getacoder.com – web design, writing, programming, ETC
15) Taskcity.com – programming
16) Clickworker.com – online marketing, e-commerce, media, information etc
17) xplace.com – designing, programming, writing/editing, translating, marketing,
18) ifreelance.com – proof-reading, arts, data entry, graphic designing, photos
19) Project4hire.com – programming, translation, consulting, graphic design

20) Scribendi.com – editing and proofreading
21) Gofreelance.com – general
22) Freelancesuccess.com -writing
23) Joomlancers.com – everything Joomla CMS related
24) Genuinejobs.com – telecommuting
25) freelancedesigners.com – web and graphic design, programming, logos
26) Governmentbids.com – general
27) Freelancers.net – general
28) Greatlance.com – general
29) Freelancer-job.com – programming
30) Wordpressfreelance.com – WordPress projects
31) outsourcexp.com – SEO, programming; engineering, admin, marketing...
32) freelancefree.com – general
33) directfreelance.com – writing, graphic design, programming
34) hourly.com – general
35) Writerlance.com – writing
36) whichlance.com – general
37) programmingbids.com – programming, databases, graphic design. 38) Maglance.com – programming
39) freelancejobsearch.com – web & graphic design, photography
40) Peopleperhour.com – programming, design, admin tasks, accounting, PR

You can get started with a few of these and see the vast potential that lies therein. These are all bidding sites. You find a job that meets your preferences and then make your bid and give an estimated time of completion. If the project poster finds that to be all right, they will select you. You are paid through online routes.

The drawback here is that you have to spend time.

You have to be at your desktop for all the time that you are generating money, which is a very different thing from other approaches such as affiliate marketing. You earn only as much as you work and there is no scope for residual income.

CHAPTER 4

DIGITAL BUSINESS GOLDMINE #4: ARTICLE WRITING

If you're good with words and writing interests you, it is possible for you to make money writing online. There are many websites just waiting to PAY you for writing articles. Also, many site owners and publishers are looking for people to write articles for them to use in promoting their businesses. Good writers can never lack for money on the internet if they know where to go and how to go about it

In case you are wondering how it is possible to be paid for writing articles online, here are 21 of the top sites where you can get paid for writing articles

CHAPTER 4B

LIST OF 30 MAJOR SITES THAT WILL PAY YOU FOR YOUR ARTICLES

1. Squidoo.com
Squidoo is a publishing platform and community where you can share personal write-ups through their website. Articles on Squidoo are called 'lenses' or pages. Once you've posted a lens, ads of similar or recommended products of what's written is placed around your lens.

The ads will consist of products which are sold via their affiliate programs with Amazon, eBay and a few others. You keep half of whatever Squidoo makes off your lens which is then payable to you via PayPal or donated to a charity for you.

2. HubPages.com
Like Squidoo, in HubPages, you write 'hubs' or articles about an original and useful topic. Once you've posted

your article, ads related to what you wrote are placed. These ads are generated from Google AdSense, HubPages Ad Program and/or affiliate programs such as Amazon and eBay products.

Once your article(s) earns the minimum amount on Google AdSense ($100) or HubPages Ad Program ($50), you can chose to cash out through PayPal.

3. ContentBLVD.com

ContentBLVD connects blog owners to writers. To be a writer for ContentBLVD, you have to send in an application and meet its criteria. Once you get in, you can start writing articles based on the topics or assignments as required by ContentBLVD's clients.

If your content gets used, you will be paid ranging from $12 to $48 per piece. For now, ContentBLVD is still in beta mode (at the time of this writing) but it is worth checking out if you want to quit writing spam assignments.

4. Helium.com

Helium is a writing community where you can choose to write about your own topic or write for one of Helium's clients under their assignment dashboard. One way to earn money through Helium is with their assignment-based articles which are sold to publishers or brands that need content for their sites and products.

You can also earn money via their Ad Revenue Sharing program where they pay you based on the amount of traffic your personal article brings to their site. You can cash out after earning the minimum of $25.

5. Triond.com

Triond is another writing community where you write articles that are then posted on other popular websites. Triond allows you to post audio, video and pictures together with your written articles which are then published to relevant websites based on what you've written.

You can then track your article views, comments and earnings via your user dashboard. You can cash out 50% of the advertising earnings from your articles every month.

6. Epinions.com

If you love writing reviews (and who doesn't?), check out Epinions. You can write positive or negative reviews about products available for purchase on web stores all over the internet. From the reviews, you earn Eroyalties credits through the Income Share program, which is redeemable in US dollars.

The program rewards reviewers who help other buyers make their decisions on buying or not buying the product based on your review. US residents can redeem their check with a minimum balance of $10 while non-US residents must have a minimum balance of $100.

7. Fiverr.com

Fiverr is a place you where you can 'sell' your writing skills or services (among others) for a fixed price of $5 – you get to keep $4. When someone buys whatever you're offering to sell, they'll pay to Fiverr first. Once you've completed the task at hand, $4 will be credited into your account. You can then withdraw your earnings via PayPal. Unlock 'levels' by selling more and more often on Fiverr, and more opportunities and tools will be opened for your use.

8. Yahoo! Contributor Network [contributor.yahoo.com]

Writers can sign up for free to be a Yahoo! Contributor where you can find daily 'assignments' to write about. Many of these assignments offer up-front payments ranging from $2 to $25 (and sometimes more). Otherwise, you can create and earn from your own content as well, with payments ranging from $2 to $15.

All payments are processed through PayPal. The content you write is shared on other Yahoo subdomains like Yahoo! News, Shopping, Voices, Sports, etc which gives you very good exposure.

9. DemandMediaStudios.com

You need to apply to write for Demand Media Studios but once accepted; you'll be given tasks or assignments which they require you to write about. These assignments will be based on subjects you are interested in or have knowledge of. This is determined when you first apply for the assignment.

We also have reason to believe that content on eHow originates from here, giving you and your articles even more exposure. Your articles that get published will net you from $15 to more than $30.

10. DigitalJournal.com
Digital Journal is a community with a rather serious tone. You can contribute by creating blog posts and interacting with groups by discussing and debating the latest news and important blogs. The more you contribute, and the more attention you bring to your post, the more you can earn from the site.

Payments are done via PayPal. In order to begin contributing, you must apply to be a Digital Journalist by submitting a sample of your writing. For more details on how this works, hear it straight from the horse's mouth.

11. About.Com
About.com is a renowned website which you've probably stumbled across more than once. Because they're so renowned, being a guide or topic writer means you have to apply to write for specific topics.

You'll also have to go through a two-part orientation and evaluation program to learn of their editorial standards before being accepted to write for them. There is no mention about how much you can earn from writing for them but payments are done on a monthly basis.

12. Blogging.Org

This is a website for people to buy and also write articles to be sold. To earn money from Blogging.org, all you have to do is contribute quality articles of specific topics. Since the other half of the website is for people to browse and purchase content, if your article gets chosen, you'll get paid a certain amount.

Articles go for as low as $1.50 up to $20 per piece, however there is no mention on how much you are entitled to. Premium writers are mentioned to 'earn $30/hour and payments are done weekly. Register for free to start writing.

13. Constant-Content.com

Constant Content is a website that allows writers to get their content sold to multiple clients. There is also a Public Request System where writers can submit fresh articles to buyers who are looking for content on a specific subject.

As you write more, you can join the Writer Pool to claim exclusive projects from clients. This is a great way to build your portfolio. Each article price is determined and paid by the client; Constant Content will take 35% while the writer receives 65% through PayPal.

14. Bukisa.com

Bukisa's aim is to give knowledge to others by sharing experiences. So most of their articles are 'How-To' guides. This is a great place to write about a something you are interested or have knowledge in.

Earnings are based on Google AdSense within your article. It's also a community where you can meet other writers. It's free to sign up so just give it a go.

15. ContentRow.com

Content Row is a company that sells content written by you. However, their FAQ states that each content written is only sold to 1 customer and the customer can use their name instead of yours on the article. Technically you sell off your right of ownership to the content you produce.

However, you will earn 50% of whatever the customer pays and can write articles that are of interest to you. To be an author for Content Row, you'll have to send in an application with 3 writing samples.

16. ArticleTeller.com

At ArticleTeller, you can be a writer for many customers

who go to their site looking to purchase content. As a writer, you can earn stars as you write each article. These starts let you move through four writing levels or rankings. You can earn more money per article if you're higher ranked.

A Requester (buyer) will pay you a certain amount for the number of words you write, and you get to keep 81% of whatever they paid for the article, payable via PayPal.

17. Xomba.com

Xomba is a place with articles in the categories of Entertainment, Home, Writing, Science & History, News & Politics, Technology and Living. Ads from Google AdSense are automatically placed on the article you write.

Despite the flexibility of topics to write on, when it comes to payments, Xomba splits the earnings with you; you will receive 40%. Also, earning through Google AdSense means you can only withdraw your earnings when it reaches $100.

18. Wizzley.com

Writing on Wizzley can earn you money in a few different ways. Besides earning from Google AdSense, you can show related products sold on Amazon in your article, and you will receive a commission if one of the products is sold through the writing your article.

They even allow you to use pictures for sale from AllPosters, and if they get sold from the click of your article, you get a share of the earnings. Other similar ways to earn commission include Zazzle and Chitika.

19. Zujava

Zujava refers to their articles as Leaves which cover a wide variety of categories. Google AdSense ads are placed on your articles together with their affiliates program like Amazon where you can feature products within your article. 50% of the earnings from ads and products sold are sent to you via PayPal.

20. SponsoredReviews

SponsoredReviews is a place where advertisers look for bloggers to write about their products. This is also a site for bloggers who want to sell sponsored posts on their blogs.

Advertisers who go to Sponsored Reviews have their own requirements for what they want in each post. Once your account and profile is on Sponsored Reviews, advertisers will visit your blog and if they're interested to buy 'advertising space', they'll contact you. Bloggers can also approach advertisers directly.

21. InfoBarrel.com

This is a fantastic money site for authors and it shares out about 75% of income to the site to the content writers

22. BreakStudios.com

You can contribute content to Break Studios and make money writing. They provide you the titles for each article and you write the content. Once your article is approved & published you will be notified and will be paid via PayPal at the end of every month. Your articles will be published on highly trafficked Break Studios' websites including Break.com, MadeMan.com, HolyTaco.com, CagePotato.com, ScreenJunkies.com & Chickipedia.com.

23. WiseGEEK.com

WiseGEEK offers free and clear answers to common questions in almost all niches (500+ topics). They pay writers per article. Currently wiseGEEK pay $10 to $14 depending on the article. You get paid via PayPal and there is no fee as they cover the PayPal fees.

24. eCopywriters.com

eCopywriters hires copywriters to assist their clients in creating quality content. They're looking for only professional copywriters only. You can earn up to $25 per hour for basic writing projects. They have different levels of writers and top level writers earn as much as $0.30 per word. eCopywriters' projects include TV & Radio Commercials, SEO Content, Blogs, Press Releases, Ads, Sales Letters, Business Letters & Plans and more.

25. LoveToKnow.com

If you're from US then you can contribute high quality articles in the niche Money & Finance, Shopping,

Fashion, Beauty, Technology, Home Improvement etc. to LoveToKnow and they pays an upfront payment for your article. LoveToKnow offers the most useful information on the topics you want to know more about.

26. Seed.com
Seed by AOL is an open content submission platform that is looking for content writers from US. AOL Network with over 100 million monthly visitors & billions of page views covers 80+ topics and you will be paid a flat fee if they acquire an exclusive license to your work or they will share the revenue with you for all the approved articles.

27. QualityGal.com
QualityGal is a content creation service dedicated to providing their clients with the highest quality SEO content. QualityGal accepts writers from all over the world and pays at least $12 per article (average of $12 and a maximum of $30) depending upon the quality of content. Payment for completed and accepted articles is made via PayPal or Check every week.

28. Textbroker.com
This is another great site that allows you to earn money for writing. If you are looking for simpler articles and writing projects, then this might be a better fit for you. You can typically earn $3.00-$8.00 an article but the articles are shorter and much easier to write in my opinion. Textbroker allows entrepreneurs and

companies the opportunity to post writing projects in the system. You go through the system and claim articles in areas of interest. They pay twice a month by PayPal on all of the articles that you have written.

29. Jobs.ProBloggerJob.net

This is more like a job board for writers but it is very good. You can find fresh, new job postings almost every day. If you are looking for some extra work, then keep your eye out on this job board. For example, if you like sports, it is not uncommon to find an opening every once in a while for a sports blogger who can write on recent sporting events.

30. FreelanceWritingGigs.com

This is a great website on many different levels. Not only can you learn how to be a freelance writer, but they have relevant, fresh job postings listed daily as well. There is even a post that list 50+ places that you can get paid for writing.

CHAPTER 4C

TOP 50 ARTICLE DIRECTORIES IN THE WORLD (By Alexa and Google Traffic Pagerank)

Apart from getting paid directly to write articles, you can also submit your articles on article directories to promote yourself as well as your businesses and products with backlinks. The more people that read your articles, the more name recognition you have and the more you attract traffic to your sites and blogs to make more sales!

Here is a list of the top articles directories in the world where you can post your articles

URL	Alexa Rating	Google Pagerank
1. ehow.com	277	7
2. hubpages.com	534	6
3. examiner.com	543	8
4. squidoo.com	667	7
5. ezinearticles.com	674	6
6. seekingalpha.com	913	7
7. technorati.com	1,760	8
8. apsense.com/article/start	2,424	4
9. goarticles.com	2,831	2
10. articlesbase.com	3,016	6
11. buzzle.com	3,580	6
12. textbroker.com	5,866	4

13. selfgrowth.com — 6,333 — 6
14. amazines.com — 7,146 — 4
15. sooperarticles.com — 9,501 — 4
16. biggerpockets.com/articles — 10,166 — 4
17. articlesnatch.com — 11,135 — 5
18. knoji.com/articles/ — 11,323 — 3
19. articletrader.com — 11,595 — 5
20. triond.com — 11,679 — 5
21. brighthub.com — 12,200 — 6
22. thefreelibrary.com — 12,621 — 7
23. suite101.com — 12,657 — 6
24. gather.com — 12,661 — 6
25. articlecity.com — 13,204 — 5
26. ezinemark.com — 13,461 — 4
27. isnare.com — 13,981 — 5
28. infobarrel.com — 14,066 — 4
29. articlerich.com — 15,415 — 4
30. EvanCarmichael.com — 15,941 — 4
31. articledashboard.com — 16,218 — 5
32. artipot.com — 16,537 — 3
33. articlesfactory.com — 17,261 — 4
34. pubarticles.com — 17,630 — 4
35. articlecube.com — 17,932 — 4
36. articlealley.com — 18,009 — 4
37. articlebro.com — 19,149 — 1
38. upublish.info — 20,151 — 4

39. thewhir.com/find/articlecentral 21,210 5
40. abcarticledirectory.com 23,765 3
41. submityourarticle.com/articles/ 23,837 3
42. helium.com 24,630 5
43. earticlesonline.com 26,555 2
44. articlecell.com 27,448 2
45. xgbook.com 27,831 4
46. a1articles.com 28,164 4
47. informationbible.com 28,716 2
48. articlesxpert.com 28,881 4
49. articlestars.com 29,261 3
50. web-source.net 29,490 6

CHAPTER 5

DIGITAL BUSINESS GOLDMINE #5: OFFLINE INTERNET CONSULTANCY

With the explosion in internet usage and patronage, being an offline internet consultant is going to a huge for many Internet marketers in the coming months and years.

While it may sound difficult to think of yourself as an Offline Internet Business Consultant, it's not really difficult to transform yourself into an offline consultant by offering your knowledge, skills and insight about marketing online to local brick and mortar companies.

With the entire buzz about internet marketing out there, many business owners already recognize the importance of being online, but they have no idea how to get there. They're just waiting to find someone to lead the way. That someone may be you!

So who's an Offline Internet Business Consultant? An offline consultant is basically someone who works with local businesses, offline, to teach, guide, counsel and assist them in bringing their businesses online. An offline consultant shares his/her knowledge of Internet marketing, website design, promotion, search engine optimization (SEO), online advertising strategies and other key concepts with local businesses who needs help... for a price.

Most Internet Marketers make a mistake of thinking that because they spend most of their time online, that the same is true of other businesses. As you get involved in building website, It easy to assume or think that every business in the world already has a website too, but that's really not the case. There are still untold multitudes of businesses--especially local ones—who don't have a viable Internet presence. And that means opportunities for you! You can take your online skills and help these business owners create a profitable online presence.

The funny thing is many business owners may not even realize they need an Internet presence. They may mistakenly believe that only large companies or companies who want to sell products online need websites. As an offline consultant, you can help them understand how Internet visibility will help their bottom line.

When it comes to establishing an internet presence, many local business owners are absolutely clueless about where to start. You, being their local marketing expert, can be their guide. You can help them understand concepts such as:

- Why Internet marketing is necessary for any business
- How to set up a website
- How to make an existing website mobile friendly
- How to optimize the site for SEO
- How to market using articles, Google ads, and more
- How to turn website visitors into cash
- How to do effective customer service using the internet
- How to use the internet to manage their corporate reputation

As an offline consultant, you may decide to be a generalist, offering help in any realm of Internet marketing, or you may specialize in certain aspects of doing business online such as website design or online promotion. You also might choose to specialize within a particular industry such as day cares, hair salons, doctors or dentists.

Today, whatever part of offline internet consulting that sounds most appealing to you, can be turned into a profitable internet consulting business. Our market is still largely under-served compared to other continents.

Here are some common services you can offer to local businesses for good money with websites like Fiverr; Odesk or Freelancer where they can actually get them done for ridiculously low amounts. You can take the deal and then outsource it to those micro job sites for peanuts while pocketing most of the money!

Another student just got a deal to build a website for a client at $1,000 though we were able to get that same website built on a template theme on Fiverr for $5!

Some of the offline consultancy deals still hot include the following:

- Internet Consultation (you offer to give this free to get a foot in the door)
- SEO Listing Services
- Website Optimization Services
- Affordable Effective Website Solutions / Graphic
- Pay Per Click Advertising
- Article & Press Release Marketing
- Video Marketing
- Social Media Marketing

- Virtual Assistant Services to manage their online platforms

Strengths: Everyone can get into the business by doing some training. There are resources available online to help you provide excellent service to your clients even if you yourself do not know much about any of those services. You can do this business straight from your suitcase or your cell phone without needing any other materials.

Weaknesses: It involves real work constantly and marketing offline which most internet marketers do not want to do. Internet marketing is typically a solo operation. The majority of interaction is done via email, online forums, blogs or social networks such as Twitter or Facebook. Offline consulting, on the other hand, involves in-person encounters with real people. If you don't like talking to people directly or on the phone, this may not really be for you.

Opportunities: The market for internet business consultants is only just beginning. In the land of the blind, the one-eyed man is king. With little knowledge you can capture big clients and charge figures that will make the experts in America and Europe green with envy.

Threats: With the realization of the huge opportunities in this business, many experts are now targeting local customers. As more and more local business consultants target local business, the niche is becoming more competitive. The good news however is that this market is so huge there will always be something for every player in the niche.

RESOURCE FOR THE SERIOUS digger
You can get certified as an Offline Internet Business Consultant by learning all it takes to be a successful offline consultant. You will get the training; tools; resources and credible certification that will enable you compete in this big niche of internet business. Click HERE to get information and find out how you can become a CERTIFIED OFFLINE BUSINESS CONSULTANT by the American Internet Business School

CHAPTER 6

DIGITAL BUSINESS GOLDMINE #6: ONLINE NETWORK MARKETING

Use Network Marketing To Generate a Waterfall of Income Beyond Your locality

If network marketing is your cup of tea, then you can learn to explore new opportunities by promoting network marketing programs on the Internet. With the internet, the possibilities for finding lucrative opportunities and recruiting downlines beyond your physical location become infinite.

With proper training and knowledge in Online Network Marketing, you can finally stop harassing your family and friends to join your MLM and instead use the power of the internet to reach beyond your country, into the world at large to recruit people who are really looking for what you have to sell.

Strengths: Similar to affiliate marketing, you don't need to see anybody and promote your programs online. You are no longer limited to your village, town or country. You have the entire world's Internet users as your prospects for your downline groups.

Weaknesses: Building a network marketing business online is prone to being impersonal. Make sure you do not adopt a 'build and burn' mentality.

Opportunities: You can easily recruit more people online compared to doing something offline (where you are limited by time and space)

Threats: Globalization – downlines are not as loyal as they used to be due to the abundance of opportunities available on the Internet.

The concept is too darned simple – you build a network of people and jointly you promote a product or service. At the same time, you try to bring more people into the network. For each person that joins the network, the Upline members earn a commission. Direct sales bring in the money too, but the main commission is brought in through the commissions that the network building generates.

However, the implementation is not quite as simple. Building the network can be formidable to most people. Even so, there are many facilities you get so that you can build the network well.

You get a website from the network marketing company that you join, you can attend physical seminars and webinars and you have access to a host of material, online and offline, where you can learn how to promote your network to the hilt.

You need to remember one thing – joining a network marketing opportunity could be a life-changing experience. You might begin seeing everything in a totally new light. But that's the way you can earn all those six figure incomes a month.

Two of the most popular network marketing opportunities of the world, Forever Living and Herbalife promote themselves on a global level. Joining such opportunities carries the great benefit of prevailing goodwill that you can cash upon. Also, they have their own training and orientation programs all over the world which can help you start out on the right foot.

The drawback here is that there are a lot of players in the network marketing (also called multilevel marketing or simply MLM) world. A lot of them are scammers and these are the people who have given the industry a bad name.

You have to particularly beware of pyramid schemes in which people earn only through building a network but don't have any product to sell. In most parts of the world, pyramid schemes are considered to be illegal and the people involved in such an activity could be prosecuted by the law.

How To Choose The Right Internet-Based Network Marketing Company

Successful online Network Marketing has NOTHING to do with selling your prospects on your company's products. What you think of as your company's product is NOT its real product at all.

Your company's real product is its TRAINING AND MARKETING SYSTEM.
- The easier and more effective the marketing and the stronger the training your company provides the easier your business will duplicate itself
- Lots of network marketers fail because the marketing methods and approach they are taught does NOT work most of the time
- You need to a great marketing system to succeed in internet and offline marketing system

Now, let us look at **7 things your internet based MLM system MUST have** for you to achieve marketing success

1. The MLM Company Must Have A Great Replicated Site With A Lead Capture Page Designed Specifically For Your Network Marketing Company.

- Capture page must have great sales copy related to the opportunity your company represents
- It Must give an incentive for people to opt in to review the opportunity

2. The Company Must Have a Free Video or Report or Brochure Designed For Your Network Marketing Company's Opportunity

- Report or Brochure should explain the features and benefits of joining your MLM opportunity
- Must focus on the support and resources available to the recruit to new distributors
- Must explain the company's products and compensation plan
- Report/Brochure should include testimonials from successful people in the company

3. The Company's System Must Have AN EMAIL FOLLOW-UP SYSTEM

- Most people don't act immediately after they have opted to review your opportunity or report
- Most people must see a marketing message at least 7 times before they take any action
- Your company must have follow-up system of

auto responding emails that continually market your leads for you
- These emails should have professionally done and strongly worded sales copy

4. The Company Must Have A Feedback System That Uses The Fear Of Loss.
- More people buy out of fear of loss than out of prospect of gain
- The company's marketing system must Invoke fear in prospects that they may forever lose commission on a new prospect if they do not upgrade
- The Company's system must show them there are negative financial consequences if they don't take action now

5. The Company Must Have A Good Product Or Service People Really Want

- While people join MLM because of dreams of making money, the Product still has to be good to sustain the business long term
- Product must service a useful purpose that meets a genuine demand
- Product should be capable of selling even if there is no compensation plan attached

6. The Company Must Provide A Strong Internet Support For Its Distributors

- Good training system that is available to new distributors
- Customer service must back up the efforts of distributors
- Incentives and Competitions must be introduced often to stimulate energy and competition

7. Your Company Must Have A Compensation Plan That Puts Money In Distributor's Pockets Quickly

- Network Marketing is sold as a means to quick financial freedom
- You Must look at the Comp Plan of Your company be sure it has something in there to put money in people's pocket quickly
- You want to look closely at the FAST-START BONUS of your company. It must be huge enough to put money in new distributors pockets quickly
- Things are moving too quickly these days. If people do not see money quickly, they are gone!

There are many great internet based mlm companies out there now that meet these critical criteria for success and you can find them on google or any of the search engines or even on Facebook!

RESOURCE FOR THE SERIOUS:

For a free resource on the -Success Secrets of internet based Network Marketing superstars, you can download my BOOK, "The Secrets Of MLM Diamonds EXPOSED" HERE. This is a $37 book but you can download a FREE COPY now while it is still available if this is an area that interest you

CHAPTER 6A

LIST OF THE 100 HOTTEST INTERNET-BASED MLM COMPANIES OF 2013

For those who are interested in making MLM their niche for their internet business, I have taken the trouble to get a list of the hottest MLM companies of 2013 from MLMRankings.com with a percentage of how much percentage increase they gained in 2013 to reflect how hot they are right now...

It should be very easy to find them on the internet just by search for their websites on google.

1   Legal Shield   1,022% Gain

2   WCM777   967% Gain

# 3	Xplocial	904% Gain
# 4	Stream Cosmetics	561% Gain
# 5	Rippln	514% Gain
# 6	wakeupnow	458% Gain
# 7	MyFunLIFE	242% Gain
# 8	Shopping Sherlock	150% Gain
# 9	MULTI-PURE	145% Gain
# 10	SoZo	141% Gain
# 11	Motives Cosmetics	99% Gain
# 12	Skinny Body Care	80% Gain
# 13	LifePath Unlimited	71% Gain
# 14	FM Cosmetics	69% Gain
# 15	Javita	63% Gain
# 16	Team National	61% Gain
# 17	H2O at Home	60% Gain
# 18	Ampegy	59% Gain
# 19	Boresha Coffee	57% Gain
# 20	The Customer Advantage	57% Gain
# 21	Trevo	55% Gain
# 22	Younique	55% Gain

# 23	Vorwerk USA	54% Gain
# 24	Syntek Global	53% Gain
# 25	Ruby Ribbon	50% Gain
# 26	Salu International	47% Gain
# 27	efusjon	41% Gain
# 28	Dove Chocolate Discoveries	40% Gain
# 29	SevenPoint2	40% Gain
# 30	Damsel in Defense	40% Gain
# 31	Linen World	40% Gain
# 32	Strong Future International	38% Gain
# 33	RBC Life	37% Gain
# 34	FUN Unlimited	35% Gain
# 35	Apriori Beauty	35% Gain
# 36	Oriflame USA	35% Gain
# 37	Demarle at Home	34% Gain
# 38	Norwex	34% Gain
# 39	Primerica	33% Gain
# 40	Private Quarters	32% Gain
# 41	Ameriplan Dental Care	32% Gain

# 42	South Hill Designs	32% Gain
# 43	Plexus Slim	31% Gain
# 44	Wine Shop at Home	31% Gain
# 45	Rodan and Fields	31% Gain
# 46	Scentsy	31% Gain
# 47	LifePharm Global	28% Gain
# 48	Synergy Worldwide	28% Gain
# 49	Creative Memories	27% Gain
# 50	Uppercase Living	27% Gain
# 51	Zurvita	26% Gain
# 52	Omnitrition International, Inc.	26% Gain
# 53	Numis Network	25% Gain
# 54	AMERICAN LONGEVITY	24% Gain
# 55	Clever Container	23% Gain
# 56	Market America	23% Gain
# 57	Seacret Direct	22% Gain
# 58	Max International	20% Gain
# 59	PartyLite	20% Gain
# 60	Savings Highway	19% Gain

# 61	Chez Ami	19% Gain
# 62	Yoli	19% Gain
# 63	HealthyCoffee	18% Gain
# 64	PartyGals	18% Gain
# 65	Home and Garden Party, Ltd.	17% Gain
# 66	Young Living Essential Oils	16% Gain
# 67	Perfectly Posh	16% Gain
# 68	Regal Ware, Inc.	15% Gain
# 69	Abundant Health Ltd	15% Gain
# 70	Celebrating Home	14% Gain
# 71	Homemade Gourmet	14% Gain
# 72	5LINX	14% Gain
# 73	USBORNE Books at Home	14% Gain
# 74	Genesis Pure	13% Gain
# 75	Nu Skin Enterprises	13% Gain
# 76	JGO	12% Gain
# 77	Level One Network	12% Gain
# 78	Xooma Worldwide	12% Gain
# 79	Xango	11% Gain

# 80	BIOPRO Technology	11% Gain
# 81	Avon	10% Gain
# 82	Pink Papaya	10% Gain
# 83	Herbalife International	10% Gain
# 84	Ignite	9% Gain
# 85	Simply Said	9% Gain
# 86	Rastelli Direct	9% Gain
# 87	TelexFree	9% Gain
# 88	Viridian Energy	9% Gain
# 89	VIVIANE	9% Gain
# 90	Thirty-One	8% Gain
# 91	Tastefully Simple	8% Gain
# 92	LifeVantage	7% Gain
# 93	Premier Designs	7% Gain
# 94	VITAMIN POWER, INC.	7% Gain
# 95	Carico International	7% Gain
# 96	Purse Party	7% Gain
# 97	Gano Excel	7% Gain
# 98	Varolo	7% Gain

99   Conklin Company   6% Gain
100 Jordan Essentials   6% Gain

CHAPTER 7

DIGITAL BUSINESS GOLDMINE #7:
NICHE MARKETING

Build a Niche Content Site to provide information and service to a motivated small group with passion in a narrow area

Niche marketing is a term people use to refer to niches that people can target to make money online without focusing on 'business opportunity' or 'make money' niches (like Internet marketing or network marketing).

It targets niches such as Self-Improvement, Dog Training, Gaming, Movies or other things that do not fall into the category of money making niches.

Strengths: You can focus on your passion and become an expert in it. Let's say you are an expert at mountain biking, then talk all about it and monetize from this niche alone.

Weaknesses: You have to be plan everything and make sure your traffic is quite targeted and an expert at it. Different niches yield different results.

Opportunities: Niche marketing opportunities are ENDLESS. All you need to do is find a niche you can excel in that nobody else is targeting (of course, this is very rare but a lot of niches are not that congested).

Threats: An untapped niche is rare – so most people go for rarer sub-niches

Suggested Course Of Action: Do a search on Google for "YOUR NICHE" FORUM (Example: if you are targeting the gaming niche, type in "gaming forum") this will be your market!

A niche content site is a site that panders to a particular group of people.

Like gardening is a niche; cooking is a niche; motor repair is a niche. Other people would not be interested in reading about these topics. But, people who are interested in these topics will surely throng your website and even come repeatedly to look for new information that you must put up all the time.

There can be a niche within a niche. Like, in gardening, there could be a sub-niche of how to do away with aphids or how to use the right mix of fertilizers to make those grapes bigger. These are sub niches. You must remember one thing here… the narrower you are making your niche, the lesser is the number of people

You are getting people for your site, but at the same time, these people are more focused and they will be more interested in doing business with you.

Think about it: If someone really wants to have some information on aphid removal, they are not going to find too many sites on it. If your site has that content and also promotes some product relating to it, like an aphid spray, the likelihood of that visitor buying the product from your site is indeed high.

This is the way you need to go about it.
- First, think of a popular niche that you would like to build a site on.

- You can you your internet research at places like Google Trends; Yahoo or Amazon to check out what many people are looking for.

- Build content. You will need to have at least 50 pages or so of content to make some kind of impact. Spruce up this content by using right keywords so that it reaches out to the people who are looking for the specific information.

- Then, look for products on your affiliate network site to promote on your niche site. Refer to chapter 1 on how to become a member of an affiliate network site. You can put ads in the form of text and banners.

- By having your own site, you are saving money on advertising services such as Google AdWords. You have to popularize your site so that more people visit, which in turn will increase the number of clicks (and sales) that you get. At the same time, the popularity of your ads will increase the prospect of your website.

CHAPTER 7A

LIST OF 160 MOST PROFITABLE NICHES FOR NEPRENEURS

Obviously there are thousands and thousands of niches and sub-niches that you can get involved with as an internet marketer.

Find below my recommend 40 hottest niches as of end of 2013 as well as some 120 evergreen niches for your review. Pick a couple out and start digging for your own gold!

TOP 40 HOTTEST MONEY-SPINNING NICHES

1. Home based businesses,
2. <u>Make</u> Money Online
3. Real estate investors & flippers.
4. Weight Loss.
5. Credit Repair
6. Debt consolidation.
7. Herbal Supplements.
8. Dating.
9. Business Opportunity Seekers in MLM
10. Attracting Women, attracting men
11. Law of Attraction
12. Golf
13. Guitar
14. Gamblers with money problems
15. Day traders
16. People needing pain relief: Head, back, tooth
17. Job hunters
18. Foreclosures
19. Settle taxes with the IRS
20. Divorce
21. DUI
22. Sales & marketing information
23. Saving Relationships
24. Affairs
25. Pets
26. Payday loans
27. Professional exam prep
28. Getting laid off from work
29. Sexual problems
30. Fertility problems
31. Stress management / anxiety
32. Last minute gifts
33. Parents with Kids with legal problems

34. Drug tests
35. Selling a home
36. Poker
37. Online gambling
38. Bankruptcy
39. Grant Money
40. College Financial Aid

120 EVERGREEN NICHES THAT YOU CAN DO

As a way of helping you identify profitable niches, I have listed below a list of over 100 EVERGREEN NICHES on internet marketing. These are niches that have stood the test of time and which will be there for a long time unlike niches that are ordinary fads, here today, gone tomorrow.

As a Netpreneur, if you are going to focus on a niche for your internet business, it is best to focus on some evergreen niches, like some of the ones listed below, so that you don't have to keep re-creating your products every year like you may have to do with 'flighty niches'

1.) ADHD
2.) Acne
3.) Adoption
4.) Alzheimer's
5.) Anger Management
6.) Anti Aging
7.) Antiquing
8.) Anxiety
9.) Archaeology
10.) Arthritis
11.) Asthma
12.) Astronomy
13.) Back Pain
14.) Backpacking
15.) Bass Fishing
16.) Become A Nurse
17.) Bird Training/Train Your Bird to Talk
18.) Boating & Sailing
19.) Bowling
20.) Boxing
21.) Camping and Hiking
22.) Ceramics
23.) Cheerleading
24.) Chess
25.) Chicken Coops
26.) Chronic Fatigue
27.) Classic Cars
28.) Cooking/Recipes
29.) Copywriting
30.) Cure Hemorrhoids
31.) Decorating
32.) Depression
33.) Diabetes

34.) Divorce
35.) Dog Training
36.) Dropshipping
37.) Eating Disorders
38.) Gambling
39.) Gardening
40.) Get Your Ex Back
41.) Golf
42.) Golfing
43.) Greenhouses
44.) Hair Loss
45.) Headaches
46.) Heart Disease
47.) Hiking
48.) Honeymoons
49.) Horse Racing
50.) Horses Training
51.) How To Be Confident
52.) How To Budget
53.) How to Get Rid of Panic Attacks
54.) How to Learn French
55.) How to Learn German
56.) How to Learn Guitar
57.) How to Learn Italian
58.) How to Learn Spanish
59.) How to Play the Piano
60.) How to Play the Violin
61.) Hunting
62.) Hypnosis
63.) Hypoglycemia
64.) Insurance (home/auto/life/pet)
65.) Interior Design
66.) Invest In Gold

67.) Knitting
68.) Landscaping
69.) Lawn Care
70.) Learn The Guitar
71.) Learn To Dance
72.) Learn To Sing
73.) Life Coaching
74.) Low Fat Recipes
75.) Magic Tricks
76.) Marriage Advice
77.) Martial Arts
78.) Massage
79.) Memory Improvement
80.) Menopause
81.) Mental Health
82.) Model Trains
83.) Motherhood
84.) Motivation
85.) Mountain Biking
86.) Multiple Sclerosis
87.) NLP
88.) Obsessive Compulsive Disorder
89.) Organic Food
90.) Parenting
91.) Photography
92.) Poker
93.) Pottery
94.) Pregnancy
95.) Psychic
96.) Psychology
97.) Public Domain
98.) Quilting
99.) Racquetball

100.) Rafting
101.) Relationships/Dating
102.) Rugby
103.) Running
104.) Saltwater Fishing
105.) Scrapbooking
106.) Scuba Diving
107.) Self-Sustainability Energy
108.) Single Parenting
109.) Skateboarding
110.) Skiing
111.) Snorkeling
112.) Snowboarding
113.) Stop Smoking
114.) [Stop Snoring](#)
115.) Surfing
116.) Swimming
117.) Tattoo Removal
118.) Tennis
119.) Time Management
120.) UFOs
121.) Volleyball
122.) Wedding Planning
123.) Wedding Speeches
124.) Weight Loss
125.) Weight Training

CHAPTER 8

DIGITAL BUSINESS GOLDMINE #8: INFORMATION MARKETING

Build a Niche Content Site to provide information and service to a motivated small group with passion in a narrow area

INFORMATION MARKETING

One of the most popular niche online – It is mostly related to teaching others how to make money online or business opportunity niches.

Strengths*:* There is a huge hungry market here looking to find the holy grail of making money online. If you have a product that can help them to make money, save money, save time, save effort or generally run their business for them, then you have a huge market here.

Weaknesses*:* This is one niche that you must make sure you produce results for your prospects. Don't be a hypocrite by telling others you can teach them to make money online but you haven't made a single cent!

Opportunities*:* There are lots of niches like resell rights, private label rights, product creation, search engine optimization and many more – you just need to find which market you are more comfortable with.

Threats*:* This is the MOST COMPETITIVE niche online – everyone is fighting for the same pie – but people are also willing to buy…

A digital product is essentially any product that you don't hold in your hands and that can be saved on a computer, smartphone or tablet.

An information product meanwhile is a product that revolves around providing information. That means something like a book, a podcast or a course.

So a digital informational product is something that ticks both these boxes… much like this very eBook! This eBook is informational because you're learning from it and it's digital because it only exists on a file on your harddrive.

Creating and selling a digital product just so happens to be one of the most popular and most effective business models that there is. The reason for this is that it offers *incredible* ROI and is highly versatile.

When you create and sell a digital product, you are providing value in the form of the information contained therein. This is what allows you to charge money for your product and it's what makes it desirable for your audience.

At the same time though, a digital product has *very* little overhead. There may be some initial investment involved in the creation of your product as you'll need to outsource the process or pay someone to create it for you but after that, you'll then be able to sell as many copies as you like without it costing you a single thing. There's no cost associated with storage, there's no delivery and there are no materials.

In business, this is known as 'COGS' or 'Cost Of Goods Sold'.

With a high value and no overheads then, a digital product can provide almost 100% profit on each sale. What's more, is that it's incredibly versatile and simple to create and sell. You don't need to get in touch with a manufacturing contractor, or find seed money, or learn to code… As long as you understand how to write into a Word processor, this option is available for *everyone*.

How People Are Making Money From Information Products

So how do you turn this into a money making business model? One good example we can turn to is 'Double Your Dating' (www.doubleyourdating.com).

Essential Dating Knowledge

Double Your Dating Book

Learn the foundation of David DeAngelo's teachings. Exact steps and specific directions to help you be more successful with women...

Attraction Isn't a Choice Book

As a man, the most important skill you will ever discover is how to trigger SEXUAL ATTRACTION inside of a...

Advanced Dating Techniques

Here you'll get intensive "boot camp style" training with step-by-step techniques for overcoming fear, approaching women, getting emails and phone...

Monthly Interviews

Every month I release one of these amazing interviews with a guy who is VERY successful with women.

This is a website that sells a wide variety of different informational products, all relating to how to attract and meet women.

The owners of this business therefore invest a little time and money into running the site and promoting it and then generate income from people who decide they would like more information and thus buy the books. This works because the products being sold have a very strong 'value proposition' which is to say that they solve a clear and simple problem and promise to make the buyers' lives better in a measurable way. This makes promotion much easier.

In this case, 'dating' is the niche (meaning the subject) and this is one of the most popular niches out there. Other popular choices include 'making money online', 'style', 'weight loss', 'muscle building'. Remember though, eBooks are just one option. You can also sell a video series, an online course, a shorter 'report' or a range of other information products.

In terms of how the business model works, it will largely be posting to a blog that will help you to bring more traffic to your website. The more you add content to your website in the form of a blog, the more people will be able to find your website via Google and the more people are likely to share your content on social media as well.

Adding content to a blog also allows you to build trust with your audience. The people who enjoy your content on the website will find themselves wanting more and trusting what you have to say. This then means they'll be far more likely to want to buy your products when they see that you provide even more information behind a small pay wall.

That right there is the basis for 'content marketing' which we'll look at more when we come onto the chapter on blogging.

Actually though, there are also other methods you can use to sell a digital product. For instance, you can sell a digital product via social media, on forums or even through Amazon (for Kindle). Another option is to let other people promote your product for you and to simply take a cut of the profits.

How to Create Your First Information Product
So there are lots of options when it comes to selling a digital product. Simply put, this is one of the simplest and easiest ways to get a product that you can then start promoting and marketing.

But how do you go about making one?

There are plenty of options here but in many cases you'll be able to simply handle the creation of your digital product yourself. If you are selling an eBook for instance then you only need to create a large MSWord document, include some images and good formatting and then save the final file as a PDF. Alternatively, if you're creating a video series, then you can just film yourself on camera and then edit the video neatly using editing software such as Adobe Photo Shop.

Creating an email course is even easier. For this, all you'll need is to write out some emails and then sign up to an autoresponder which you can use to automatically send your emails. A good choice is AWeber (www.aweber.com).

The main tip when doing this is to make sure you come up with a digital product that will play to your strengths and that you can be proud of.

It's *very* important to come up with a digital product you're proud of because that way you'll be able to promote it much more easily. When you talk about a product you truly believe in, your passion will come across and people will be far more likely to believe in what you're offering too. If you're kind of shy of the quality of what you've created, then your marketing will lack conviction and you won't attract repeat customers.

In terms of creating something that plays to your strengths, that means picking a topic that you know a lot about and that is relevant to the topic or niche of your website and it means creating something you *can* create well. If you're a great writer, then write an eBook! If you aren't so good at writing though but have an excellent manner on camera, then film a video series! If you can't do either of those things, then consider using screenshots of your computer/creating slideshows and then narrating them.

Alternatively, another popular option is to simply outsource the creation of your digital information product. There are thousands of writers, video editors and other skilled individuals on the web and any one of them will likely be happy to help.

The best places to find these people are generally freelancing sites which include the likes of 'Elance' (www.elance.com) or 'UpWork' (www.upwork.com). On either of these you should be able to find someone with the skills you need and from there it will cost you between $100 and $1,000 depending on the nature of the job you need done and the quality you are looking for (good writers will generally charge upwards of $3 per 100 words).

What To Price Your eBook?
Once you have your digital product, the next question is how much you want to charge for it. This of course is entirely up to you, though you don't want to charge too much and alienate your audience. We recommend around $7 for a short report, or $17-27 for a full length eBook (10,000 words plus).

What you'll find when you look around the web is that there are plenty of examples of eBooks being sold for ridiculous prices – sometimes as much as $50, $100 or more. While this does happen, the books very rarely manage to provide value for money and in the long run this can lead to damaged reputations and angry customers. Likewise, you'll find it much easier to sell a cheaper book to begin with until you have built up a reputation for yourself as someone who can be trusted and who delivers premium content.

A good tip is to start with something small to test the market. Don't aim to create the eBook to end all eBooks. Instead, start out with something smaller like a report and sell that for $7. This allows you to very quickly and easily start honing your business model and generating income without investing too much or creating too much risk. Only once you've seen that this method is working and you're earning money, do you then go and invest further into the business model with a bigger product at a higher price point.

Remember too – there's nothing to stop you from experimenting with price points and running 'split tests' to see which is the most profitable!

Creating Your Landing/Sales Page
One of the most important tools when it comes to affiliate marketing is to create a landing page. This is essentially a single page, also known as a 'sales page', that is entirely dedicated to selling your one product.

A sales page will look different from the other pages on a website because it has no links to other parts of the site, no adverts and no distracting images. In other words, *everything* on the page is there to serve the one objective of selling copies of your information product or whatever else it is that you're selling.

Often these pages are long and narrow and they contain a lot of text and a lot of 'buy now' buttons. Those buy now buttons are your 'call to action' buttons and of course they contain the affiliate link you just acquired.

The real magic of the landing page is the text. All the copy here is going to be aimed at persuading people to buy the product and this is where you're really going to earn your wage. Your objective is to be as persuasive as possible while not misrepresenting what you have to sell.

The way to do this is to remember that 'value proposition'. That means focusing on what the product *does* for people. How will their lives be better after they've used it? Maybe they'll be a success with the opposite sex, or maybe they'll be much richer and happier. Your job is to get them to imagine that possibility and to really desire it. At the same time, you point out their current failings in their situation and why their previous attempts to improve their lot in life may have failed. In other words, you present a problem and then provide the solution – that solution being the eBook you're selling or the online course.

An easy and fast way to create a sales page is by using OptimizePress (http://optimizepress.com) which is a theme for Wordpress.

Once you have this landing page, you'll then be well equipped to market your product very easily. For instance, if you pay for advertising then all you need to do is ensure those ads are sending the right kind of traffic to your sales page! Likewise, you can hand out flyers with the URL of your sales page, or you can mention it in social media posts. If you've written your sales script well then you can expect a large number of people who stumble on that page to end up converting – becoming paying customers!

This is such a wide area that we cannot possibly do justice to it in a book of this nature. However, if you really want to know how to get started in internet marketing as a niche, I encourage you to take a foundational course at: www.internetnewbiesacademy.com .

CHAPTER 9

DIGITAL BUSINESS GOLDMINE #9: DROP SHIPPING

Make Money Selling Physical Products As A Middleman!

Another really hot DIGITAL BUSINESS GOLDMINE is something called 'drop shipping'. Here, you are essentially acting as something between a reseller and an affiliate and you're cutting out the middle man – in this case eBay.

Drop shipping essentially involves selling products on the behalf of a wholesale supplier. You promote the product just as you normally would and then you process the payment. Then, all you do is to pass the shipping details on to the supplier and pay them their share.

In many ways, drop shipping is the *perfect* business model. You get to sell real products that appeal to a huge range of potential customers and at the same time, you don't have to worry about fulfillment or inventory. Better yet, most of your customers never need to know that you're drop shipping. 'Private label shipping' means that you get to ship the product from the wholesaler with your branding and return address on the packaging!

How to Get Started Drop Shipping
The only *downside* of drop shipping as a business model is that it can be somewhat difficult at times to find willing wholesalers who will play along. This means you may need to do some extensive searching in order to find a company that supplies what it is you're hoping to sell and that will offer the drop shipping service.

Fortunately, there are some tools you can use to more easily find drop shipping wholesalers. One is Alibaba (www.alibaba.com/) which lets you easily search through a directory of products and then find the contact details for the seller.

Another is Worldwide Brands (www.worldwidebrands.com), though that directory requires paid membership (oh look, an example of a membership site!).

Another final option, is to target the manufacturers themselves. If you find a product you really like, then just look up who made it and find their contact details. It never hurts to try!

Creating an eCommerce Store

If you're going to become a drop seller then creating an ecommerce store will be highly helpful when it comes to generating sales. What's more, an ecommerce store can *also* be very helpful when it comes to several other of these business models.

An ecommerce store is essentially an extension of your website or blog through which you can sell products. This will list your items and allow people to easily buy them and will then manage your sales – for you to pass on to your manufacturers/wholesalers.

As with creating a membership site, you can often create an ecommerce store simply by adding a plug in to your WordPress site. One of the most popular options is WooCommerce (http://www.woothemes.com/woocommerce/) which simply requires you to install the plugin to your WordPress and then start entering your items, your prices and your payment details (for receiving payments).

If you're looking for something a bit larger, then another choice is Megento (www.magento.com/). Magento works just like WooCommerce except it is *not* a WordPress plugin. This means you'll need to set up a Magento store like a separate site on your server and then point to it. In exchange, you get a much more powerful system capable of listing up to 50,000 items (whereas WooCommerce is suitable for up to 500 items).

An alternative route to go is Shopify (www.shopify.com/). Shopify is a 'hosted' solution, which means that you don't install or upload it yourself.

Instead, Shopify is like a separate website with a login and you then create a store *on* that site and then link to it from your own blog. Shopify grants you less flexibility as compared with a self-hosted solution such as WooCommerce. However, in exchange it is somewhat easier to manage seeing as it isn't 'your responsibility' as it were.

CHAPTER 10

DIGITAL BUSINESS GOLDMINE #10:
CPA MARKETING

Making Money Based On Your Site Visitor's Action

CPA marketing stands for 'Cost Per Action'. This is an interesting alternative to affiliate marketing that is similar in many ways.

Basically, what 'cost per action' means is that you get paid every time someone carries out a certain action. Now, in many cases this might mean that you get paid when someone buys something – in which case it is working similarly to affiliate marketing (except that you're getting paid a flat rate most likely). In other cases though, the 'action' might mean subscribing to a mailing list or joining a membership site.

Another difference is that CPA is often managed more similarly to PPC or display advertising. In other words, rather than promoting a product you might simply place adverts on your website. Instead of being paid for every click though, you get paid when someone clicks on the advert *and then* takes the required action.

Getting Started

Similar again to affiliate marketing, the first thing you need to do to get started with CPA marketing is to find yourself a platform where you'll be able to track down the different offers and start promoting the adverts/links.

Currently, CPA marketing isn't quite as big as affiliate marketing which is both a good thing and a bad thing. It's a good thing because it means less competition for you but it's a bad thing because it's a little harder to find good options. Likewise, there aren't as many networks that have quite risen to the top of the heap like JVZoo or Clickbank. *Some* of the CPA networks are actually a bit poorly made and in some cases even disreputable. Make sure you do your research then before choosing one to go with!

That said, some good CPA networks to choose from include Max Bounty (www.maxbounty.com), PeerFly (www.peerfly.com) or Clickbooth (www.clickbooth.com). Make sure to read the reviews and browse through what's available in order to find the right products and deals that you want to promote.

MaxBounty is a must if you want to start in CPA marketing

What you'll find when looking at these is that the whole process is a little simpler and more automated versus affiliate marketing. You simply sign up as a publisher and then post the ads/promotions on your site without having to deal directly with the brand that is offering the CPA promotion. In other words, this system is a lot closer to using AdSense or other 'Pay Per Click' adverts.

PeerFly is another great CPA network you might want to add to the list

How to Get Accepted Into a CPA Network

One of the tougher parts of CPA marketing is that you need to be 'accepted' into the network and into the specific deal.

In order to make sure that they are offering their clients the very best service, CPA networks make sure to vet the publishers they work with closely. They want to make sure that you are representing the offers you're promoting well and that the brands they work with will be proud to be associated with your business.

All this means that if you have a website that looks like it was made by a 13 year old, you're going to struggle. Likewise, if you have no prior experience or examples of your work then you may also struggle.

So the solution is to make sure that you have a good website that you can demonstrate to those networks that you're delivering good value and you're reaching a larger audience. This does mean that CPA might not be the best choice for those who are starting out with their first online business model – as they'll need to build up some traction first.

Another tip for getting accepted into CPA networks is to pick up the phone and give them a call. Ask to speak with an affiliate manager and this way you can put forward your strong case for why you think you should be accepted. This essentially fast tracks you and it's certainly much quicker and easier than waiting for lots of emails to come through.

CHAPTER 11

DIGITAL BUSINESS GOLDMINE #11: SOFTWARE VENDING

Market Software As A Service and Make Millions

Selling software is one of the most emphatic routes to make good money on the Internet. People who use computers are always trying to make their jobs easier or to add more quality to their jobs. That is the reason they look for good software all the time.

With broadband Internet, it has become so very easy to provide software in downloadable formats. You promote a link from where people can download particular software and allow them to access it when they make payment. They will pay and you give them the link to download the software.

Many marketers tease people by giving them demo versions of the software for free. This allows the downloaders to understand the quality of the product before they decide to spend good money on it. These demo versions generally have some features locked or they are timed demos which expire after an hour's worth of usage or so. When that happens, people are prompted to buy the product to make use of it limitlessly.

So, what must this software be like? People on the Internet like each and every kind of software. Or, let us put that in another way - each and every type of software on the Internet will find takers.

There's a niche for everything on the Internet. So, if you have made a software application that will help Grandma remember her recipes or made a software that will help a businessman with his end-of-the-year accounting, you are going to find people who will be willing to download that and check it out. The success lies in the promotion.

For promotion, you can use more of the same methods that you have been using all along. If your software becomes prominent, especially in places where your niche market usually visits, you could be assured of a healthy flow of downloaders. At the same time, you have to remember that there is no lifespan for this. There will always be downloaders, provided you promote well and keep upgrading your software, which means, you can keep generating a flow of passive income through this.

You do not need to have your own software application either. You could buy the resell rights of software and sell it. There are several creative people on the Internet who like building software but don't like the marketing it.

These people give away the software they have developed for a price. You can modify these software applications to an extent and in some cases you can rebrand them too. Of course, you sell them at a much higher and enduring price than you bought it for.

You could just look for 'software resell rights' on Google to find a host of such sites.

Like everything else, there are so many categories of this gold mine and those who want to play in this area have lots of choices as to the specific niche of this section they want to play at. To help you have an idea of the different software markets available to you, I have included a list of some of the most common types of software that are in his demand today. Enjoy!

How to Monetize Software
One of the most simple and straightforward ways to monetize software is of course to simply *sell* the software. This can be very varied in terms of the scope and the price.

For instance, if you look at a piece of software such as Sony Vegas (video editing software), that will set you back several hundred dollars for the full package. On the other hand, you then have 'apps' which will sell on the Google Play Store or Apple App Store for 50cents.

Of course it's much easier to go after the latter market – a small app is cheaper to develop and maintain and from there, you'll have a great route to market (and payment system) in the form of those stores.

Another option with an app meanwhile is to make money from advertising. In this model, you actually give the app away for *free* but then make money every time someone clicks on or views an ad that shows on top of it.

SaaS

Another completely different option is to go the SaaS route. This stands for 'Software As A Service' and essentially it means that you are selling access to a piece of software for a recurring fee – much like a subscription.

The dating website Match.com (www.match.com) is a great example of this. Others will often offer a free membership in order to attract potential customers and then encourage to upgrade their membership for a fee, giving access to more features. Examples of this include Dropbox (www.dropbox.com), Evernote (www.evernote.com) and Feedly (www.feedly.com).

How to Create Your Own Software

Now, creating a piece of software is going to be a little more challenging than creating an information product. The question is just how much of a challenge you're willing to take on.

If you're going to create a mobile app, then assuming it's something simple, this will require a relatively low investment and should be something most readers can accomplish. On the other hand though, if your intention is to create a SaaS business model, this will involve a lot more work.

That's because creating software that can be a service will normally mean creating something that runs in the browser and is cloud enabled. In other words, people need to be able to log in from anywhere, edit files, communicate with others, etc.

This then means that your program is going to need to run on a server, which immediately makes things more complicated as now you'll need to understand how servers work and you'll probably need multiple coding languages in order to handle what's going on behind the scenes (called the 'backend'). You'll also need to deal with customer complaints and potential errors and generally *provide a service*. This is not a passive model and it has a much larger barrier to entry.

Of course on the other hand, creating a SaaS model means that you have much more guaranteed income and potentially earn much more from each customer. Once again then, the best advice is to start with something much more simple like a mobile app and then to build up to bigger challenges such as a web app.

Either way, you're going to either need to *learn* programming or you're going to need to find someone who can help you do that. Once again, you can outsource the creation of your software by going to Elance and UpWork. If you're building a SaaS business, then note that you're going to need a 'full stack developer' which means that you're hiring someone who understands everything from HTML and CSS (which are used in web design) to PHP and Linux. In other words, they need to know every stage of the coding process and each element that contributes to a smoothly running piece of cloud software. If you can't find a true full stack developer, then you'll more likely need a team.

For mobile apps, finding a developer will be a bit simpler. Do make sure you see a sample of their work first though and for preference, try to choose someone who is in your local area so that you can work together at the same computer. This will save you a LOT of time.

Doing It Yourself

If you want to create your own software though, then what options do you have?

Unfortunately, this is a *massive* question and not one that can easily be answered here. Suffice to say that there are hundreds if not thousands of programming languages out there and the right one to learn will depend entirely on your skill level and the nature of your project. To make an Android app for instance you will need to learn Java, as well as how to use the Android SDK. Conversely, if you're making a computer game for the PC, then the easiest strategy is likely going to be learning to use Unity which will require a little coding in C#.

As mentioned, creating a web app is a huge undertaking and will require you to learn HTML and CSS along with PHP, Python or Ruby, several frameworks and more.

All this is not to say that learning to code can't be done. Just recognize that there's no single way to do it and it will take time. If you're coding yourself then you *must* start with a simple project. Buy yourself a book, do lots of Googling and work towards something very simple as a learning exercise to begin with.

Another option is to use something like an 'app builder'. These are very limited in terms of what they can accomplish though and won't be suitable for most online business models.

So this option is a little harder than the last two. Still though, if you can create something truly useful and unique then you'll have contributed greatly to the web and you can be very proud of that! And while unlikely, this has very real potential to make you very rich!

Chapter 12
DIGITAL BUSINESS GOLDMINE #12: MEMBERSHIP SITES MODEL

Make Money From Recurrent Monthly Membership Sites

So, creating a SaaS business model is a rather large undertaking compared to becoming an affiliate marketer. But as we saw, it definitely does have its advantages as well. And one of the biggest of those advantages is the fact that it allows you to set up recurring income and to earn *much* more from a single visitor. Instead of getting a one off payment for a download, you get a recurring payment from that same person for months or maybe even years.

And as it happens, there is an easier way to accomplish this… which is simply to set up a membership site! As the name suggests, this is a website or blog that charges a recurring fee for membership. Normally this works by presenting some information for free but then having more information and perhaps discussion/community behind a pay wall.

An example of this is Longe City (www.longecity.org). This is a website all about techniques you can use to live longer, or that you can use to improve your brain power using supplementation. While the main site is free and you can even read much of the forum, in order to participate in the discussion you need to become a paid member.

Another good example is Lynda.com (www.lynda.com). This site has a different topic – teaching a range of skills – but is once again a paid site meaning that you need to be a member in order to access the articles. Many newspapers with websites also do the same thing – but partly this is to avoid preventing people from paying for their papers by getting the same content online for free!

Creating Your Membership Site
The good news is that creating a membership site is really relatively simple and straightforward. All you need to do is to create a website or blog as you normally would – using WordPress (http://www.wordpress.org) and then to install a plugin that will handle the recurring fee on your behalf. These include 'AMember'

(www.amember.com) and 'MemberMouse' (http://membermouse.com/).

The hard part here then, is getting people to want to subscribe to your blog or website when they're so used to getting content online for free. In order to make it worthwhile, you're going to have to offer something that they feel they can't get elsewhere or that is more valuable than what they're used to getting for free.

Building a big community is also a great way to do this, as people love getting interaction with others who are interested in their topic and they love feeling as though they are a part of an 'exclusive' membership program. It's like being in a secret club!

The examples we looked at both do this very well. In the case of Longecity.com, you have a community discussing things that are potentially very valuable (raising IQ and life extension) and information that isn't available everywhere. This lends itself very well to the 'underground website' mentality and makes becoming a member very appealing.

Meanwhile, Lynda.com provides skills and training that someone might be able to use to earn more money. Thus they are getting real value for money and they may even be able to consider it as an investment.

Your job when creating your membership site then is to create something that is exciting, exclusive and rare so that people are willing to pay to become a part of it. And often this is going to involve giving *some* content away for free in order to demonstrate the value on offer.

YouTube

Note that there is another option available for those looking to make money from paid content. YouTube has a 'paid content' option that allows you to keep certain videos behind a pay wall. This is a great option as YouTube will make it easier for you to handle payments and to promote your content. Check out how to do this here: https://support.google.com/youtube/answer/3249127?hl=en-GB.

Conclusion and Summary

So there you have it: 12 very effective internet marketing business models (and a few others mentioned) you can start using right away to generate an income from the comfort of your home. Many of these models are passive, meaning that you can generate money while you're sleeping; others have the potential to scale to full sized businesses – anything is possible!

We've gone over an awful lot over the course of this book and have discussed a diverse range of different options. For some readers, selling a product via eBay is going to be most appealing, while others might prefer the idea of becoming an affiliate.

Either way, the very *core* of every business model is the same. Your job is to provide value to a specific target audience and to make sure that you're able to communicate directly with that audience in order to promote the product. At the same time, you need to ensure it costs you less to do this than you earn from the sales – which normally means that you have to somehow add your own value.

How to Proceed

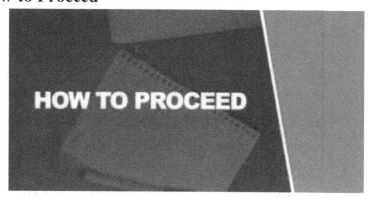

At this point you may be suffering with a little overwhelm. With so many options and so many strategies, how do you know where to start?

And some of these models involve building up a highly successful blog – so you may find that off putting.

The trick then is to make sure you start with just one model first and to start small. The key early on is to start seeing results as soon as possible. As soon as you start generating *any* income, you'll understand how the process works and you'll open up new opportunities.

In other words, you're not going to become a huge success overnight with a SaaS model – it's just too much work. But making a few bucks from selling some items on eBay? That's *super* easy and highly doable. The same goes for generating some money from selling an affiliate product.

Don't set out to change the world. In fact, don't even set out to get rich! If you do, you'll likely only be disappointed which more often than not leads to quitting. Instead, set out to just earn *some* money in a quick, safe and low-risk manner. Then set out to build on that success and to replicate the business model or add another string to your bow. Take one step at a time and do what you need to do every day to eventually reach your goals!

Look at it this way: even if you only make $30 of sales a week for the rest of your life, that's still $120 a month – or $1,440 a year! How much better would life be with that extra money? You could go on holiday guilt free!

Another tip? Always emulate the success stories. Over the course of this eBook we've looked at many cases of people who have been successful with these various business models whether it's as an affiliate marketer or a blogger. Look at what they've done, study them carefully and repeat their model. Success always leaves clues and you can follow those clues to repeat the business model.

Likewise, don't overcomplicate matters. If you *do* find a business model out there that works then there's nothing wrong with copying it! Don't make things harder than they already are because your pride gets in the way. Don't choose to build your own PHP CMS when you *could* just use WordPress.

Some affiliate products that are selling very well will *even* give you the marketing materials that the creator used to generate their sales. This is the perfect 'copy and paste' business model because you're literally taking what worked for them and doing the exact same thing within your sphere of influence. That's great – it's not breaking the mold but it's easy and it *works*. Look for those easy wins!

There's Much More!
Of course we've only really scratched the surface here as well in terms of what's possible. There are *countless* more ways to earn money online as a marketer and there's nothing to stop you from inventing your own methods either as you get more confident.

For instance, we barely touched on the option of selling your own services. If you're a web designer, a writer, a life coach or a personal trainer then creating a website and marketing it is a great way to promote those skills. Or how about promoting the services of others? You can even get into online arbitrage – in other words, selling a service and then outsourcing the process to someone else for a lower fee.

We haven't even touched on the use of 'in-app purchases' as another way to monetize a piece of software. And what about making money from video as a popular vlogger?

There are countless opportunities. So start with something simple to learn the ropes, then let your creative juices flow!

Your Action Plan

With all these different models available, it's impossible to lay out one plan that will appeal to everyone. Generally though, these are the steps you should take…

1. Think over the different business models we've discussed. Assess your current situation, your contacts and any marketing you've done in the past and identify what will work best for you.

2. Choose products and a niche that you already know about and that you're happy to work with.

3. At the same time, start as small as possible. Minimize the investment and the risk involved and focus on creating one small, easy business model that has been tried and tested.

4. This will normally involve finding an audience and providing value. That means finding your target market, finding a way to reach them and showing them the product.

5. Reinvest some of your profits into growing your business. That may mean investing in more marketing for your affiliate products, or it may mean investing in more inventory.

6. Build a website and grow it in order to generate your own audience. Eventually, this will become an excellent asset to you because it will provide

you with your own, effective route to market.

7. Either repeat the business model that has worked for you (selling one affiliate product? Time to sell two!), or branch out into the next area.

8. Keep refining and perfecting your business model and keep on growing!

So what are you waiting for? You've seen how easy it is – now go out there and start earning from one of these models!

Made in the USA
Monee, IL
19 April 2022